microprocessor systems handbook

BY

DR. D. P. BURTON

Manager, Development Engineering
Analog Devices B.V. Limerick, Ireland

DR. A L. DEXTER

Lecturer in Engineering Science
Trinity College, Dublin, Ireland

Published by
Analog Devices, Inc.
Norwood, Massachusetts 02062 U.S.A.

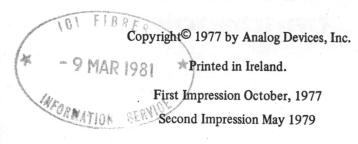

Additional copies, at $9.50, may be ordered from Analog Devices, Inc.
P. O. Box 796, Norwood, Mass 02062.

PREFACE

The intent of this book is to provide a concise explanation of microprocessor hardware, the interaction of hardware and software, and the interfacing of microprocessors with A/D and D/A converters.

It is intended as an introduction to microprocessors and as a companion to basic learning efforts employing specific devices, for which it will provide the enhancement of a generalized conceptual framework. It should be useful to engineers who require a succinct explanation of microprocessors, the related terminology, and techniques for interfacing them with the "real world," as well as to students, technicians, and scientists of all persuasions. It assumes that the reader has some knowledge of digital-system building blocks, such as counters, registers, and adders, as well as an elementary knowledge of memory circuits.

Though there are many texts that deal with the details of specific hardware and software, the need has been felt for a text providing an emphasis on systems aspects, rather than detailed circuit design, and on the broad understanding of "principles" — and the variety of ways they can be embodied.

The book was intentionally written without dwelling at length on the characteristics of any particular microprocessor, in order to make it easier to explain optional configurations and to provide necessary background for assessment and comparison of different architectures. It should be useful regardless of the type of computer the reader is using. The final chapter, for example, covers five applications, of ascending complexity, each using a different microprocessor.

The first six chapters discuss the operation of a simple microcomputer, memory addressing, input-output operations and hardware interconnection with the microprocessor, internal architecture, and memories. The last three chapters deal with A/D and D/A converters, the techniques for interfacing them to the microprocessor, and — as noted above — some examples of microprocessor aplications.

The book began as a series of lecture notes written for undergraduate courses in 1976/77 at the National Institute of Higher Education (N.I.H.E.), Limerick, and Trinity College at the

University of Dublin, in Ireland. It was edited by Dr. Peter Beevor, of the University of Dublin, and graphics are by Joe Delaney.

For the publication of this book by Analog Devices, the authors acknowledge the assistance of Heinrich Krabbe, Managing Director of Analog Devices B.V. - Ray Stata, President of Analog Devices, Inc. - and Dan Sheingold, Technical Handbooks Editor.

Limerick, 1 September 1977   *D.P. Burton*
                                               A.L. Dexter

THE AUTHORS

Dr. D. Philip Burton is Manager, of Development Engineering, at Analog Devices, B.V., in Limerick. He holds a postgraduate diploma in control systems and a Ph. D. in logic-system design.

He has consulted on radio-telescope design, was chief engineer of Infotronics, Ltd. – designing instrumentation for gas chromatography and hospital laboratories – and, most recently, as Lecturer at N.I.H.E., helped to set up a new college and courses in electronics. A thorough-going entrepreneur, he currently consults for a number of establishments in Ireland, manufactures transformers in a side business, and even owns a retail newsagent's shop – all in addition to his duties at Analog Devices.

Dr. Arthur L. Dexter is Lecturer in Engineering Science at Trinity College, at the University of Dublin. His B.A. (first class) and D. Phil. are from Oxford, he is a member of the Institute of Measurement and Control and the Institution of Electrical Engineers, and he is a Chartered Engineer. Prior to and following his doctoral dissertation, "An Investigation into the Computer Modeling of Industrial Processes," he has been engaged in a wide variety of projects in simulation, computation, and control. Some representative projects include a real-time hybrid model of the U.K.A.E.A. steam-generating heavy-water reactor, an analog interface for an IBM1130, instrumentation of an experimental boiler rig, simulation and control of the U.K. natural-gas grid, an experimental investigation into the transient thermal behaviour of a heated room, hydraulic modeling of secondary flows, and microprocessor control of domestic heating systems.

INTRODUCTION BY ANALOG DEVICES

Analog Devices, Inc., is a leading worldwide supplier of precision electronic products for use within industrial automation, process-control, medical, test-instrumentation, and avionics markets. Representative products include computer interface components (A/D and D/A converters), signal-conditioning components, and conversion instruments and systems.

Perhaps the two most important accomplishments of the low-cost microprocessor have been to vastly increase the amount of digital-processing power available to the world, and, at the same time, to disperse (rather than centralize) this power in untold numbers of new applications in systems, instruments, data processing peripherals, and personal devices for consumer, government, industrial, and service markets.

It has been estimated that some 35 percent of all microprocessor applications will involve interfacing with "real-world" (i.e., analog) data for measurement and control. Since this is exactly where Analog Devices "lives," the proper understanding by our customers — both present and prospective — of microprocessors and their application is a matter of great importance to us.

We have found this book most helpful in rounding out our own education about microprocessors, and we commend it to those who have found our products and publications helpful in the past, as well as to those with whom we expect to become acquainted in the future.

Norwood, Mass. U.S.A.   *Ray Stata*
1 September 1977

"Is feárr bheith déanach ná ró dhéanach".

Sean-Fhocal

.

(It is better late than very late.)

Old Irish Proverb

TABLE OF CONTENTS

Basic Instruction Cycle, Arithmetic and Logical Instructions, Memory Reference Instructions, Jump Instructions, Input-Output Instructions, Elementary Example of a Microcomputer Program, Use of the Index Register, Instruction Notation Methods

Arithmetic and Logical Instructions, Arithmetic Flags, Direct, Indirect and Immediate Addressing, Refinements to Memory Addressing Modes, Relative Addressing, Classical Structure of the Op-Code for Memory Reference Instructions, Memory Reference Instructions for Microprocessors, Register Addressing, Paging, On-Chip Register Addressing, Building-up Sophisticated Memory Reference Instructions, Jump and Conditional Jump Instructions, Conditional Jump Instructions, Reducing the Number of Bytes in a Jump Instruction, Subroutines, Multiple Address Machines

Program Controlled I/O, Interrupt Controlled I/O, Real-Time Operation, Example of I/O using a Real-Time Clock, Interrupt Servicing in a Multiple Interrupt System, Maintaining Program Continuity during Multiple Interrupt Service, Direct-Memory-Access I/O

Basic Types of Bus Structures, Bus Control Signals, Typical Bus Systems, Interconnecting Several Sources of Information

to the Same Bus, Interconnecting Several Acceptors of
Information to the Same Bus, The Three-State Bus, The
Memory/Bus Interface, Input-Output/Bus Interfaces

The Internal Elements of a Microprocessor Circuit, A Bit-Slice
Central Processing Element, A Basic Microprogram Control
Unit, Enhancements to the Microprogram Control Unit,
Pipelining, A Simple Example of a Microprogrammed Processor,
Multi-Chip Microprocessors

Semiconductor Memories, The Basic Read/Write Memory Cell,
Organisation of Serial-Access Read/Write Memory Arrays,
Random-Access Read/Write Memories, Content-Addressable
Read/Write Memory, User or Field-Programmable Read/Write
Memory, Read-Mostly Memory, The Programmable-Logic
Array, Uses of Memory in a Microprocessor System, The use
of Static RAM in a Volatile Read/Write Memory System, The
Use of Dynamic RAM in a Non-Volatile Read/Write Memory
System

Digital-to-Analog Conversion Using Resistive Networks, Digital-
to-Analog Conversing Using Pulse-Width Modulation, Tracking
A/D Converters, Successive-Approximations A/D Converters,
Dual-Slope Integrating-Type A/D Converters, Other types of
Integrating A/D Converters, Multi-Comparator Ladder, D/A
Converters Using Microcomputers, A/D Converters Using
Microcomputers

Digital-to-Analog Circuits and the Microcomputer Interface,
Multiple-Byte Parallel Data Transfers, Fast A/D Converters
and the Microcomputer Interface, Slow A/D Converters

and the Microcomputer Interface, Making A/D Converters
Appear as Memory, Analog Circuits in a Digital Environment,
Future Trends in Converters

Operation of a Simple Microcomputer

Chapter 1

This chapter gives a brief introduction to the basic elements which comprise a microcomputer and to the concept of an instruction set.

INTRODUCTION

A microcomputer (MPU) is a collection of digital circuit elements connected together so as to form an information processing unit. This unit is usually composed of three essential elements as shown in Figure 1-1. The system elements are a program memory which remembers or "stores" the program which the system is to execute, a data memory which is used to store the numbers which are being manipulated, and a microprocessor (MPU) which operates on the data in the sequence dictated by the program. For example, if the circuit is required to find the average value of a set of numbers, then the numbers will be stored in the data memory, the averaging program is stored in the program memory and the actual calculations will be done by the microprocessor. It is important to

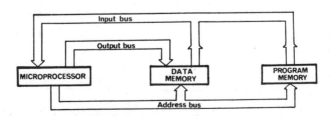

Figure 1-1. Block diagram of a simple micro-computer

recognise at this point that whilst the microprocessor is the focal point of the system, it cannot exist in isolation; there must be facilities for storing the program and there must be some sort of data storage. The program is stored in the program memory as a set of binary characters which are "coded" to represent the various steps which the microprocessor must execute. The microprocessor contains circuits which can decode those instructions and implement the prescribed program steps.

Inside the microprocessor circuit itself there are several "registers" which are used to store binary numbers of particular significance. The most important of these registers are:

(i)   *The accumulator:* often abbreviated to acc.; this is the focal point for all data manipulation. Numbers are added to or subtracted from the accumulator; often certain operations such as shift can only be done using the accumulator.

(ii)   *The index register:* this is used to store and create data addresses which are particularly important.

(iii)   *The instruction register:* in order to make the microprocessor system execute a particular program, the program memory sends a series of commands, or "instructions," to the

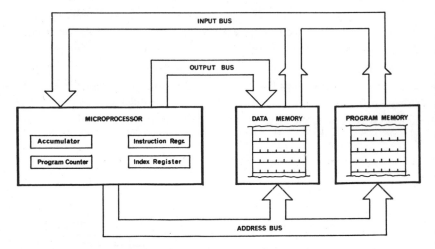

Figure 1-2. Expanded block diagram of micro-computer system showing registers and some memory cells

processor. As each instruction is received by the MPU it is stored in the instruction register. The MPU then carries out the operation required by that particular instruction before receiving the next instruction.

(iv) *The program counter:* often abbreviated to p.c.; this keeps track of the system's progress through the program. Some instructions can modify the way in which the program counter behaves.

Figure 1-2 shows a microcomputer system diagram with some of the internal registers and memory cells drawn in.

An important feature of a microcomputer system is the way in which the three basic system elements, MPU, program memory and data memory, communicate with each other by means of buses. A bus is a set of connections along which parallel binary information can be transmitted. Only one piece of parallel information (usually called a *byte*) can exist on a bus at any one time. For example, in Figure 1-2 it would not be permissible for the program memory and the data memory to simultaneously send information to the MPU via the input bus. Clearly, one of the system elements should assume control of the buses and this task usually falls to the microprocessor. Bus control is done by means of special signals generated by the microprocessor and sent out on various control lines. Sometimes these control signals are grouped together under the heading "Control bus," but this nomenclature is misleading. For clarity, the control signal paths are not shown in Figure 1-2. In the remainder of this chapter, the system connection of Figure 1-2 will be used; it will be assumed that the input bus and the output bus are both 8 bits wide and the address bus is 16 bits wide.

BASIC INSTRUCTION CYCLE

In following a program step-by-step, the microcomputer system uses the bus connections to exchange information in a well-defined manner. The complete sequence of information exchanges which carries out one program step is known as an instruction cycle. A basic cycle consists of just three events:

(i) Fetch the next instruction (i.e., program step) from the program memory to the instruction register.

(ii) Increment the program counter.

(iii) Execute the instruction.

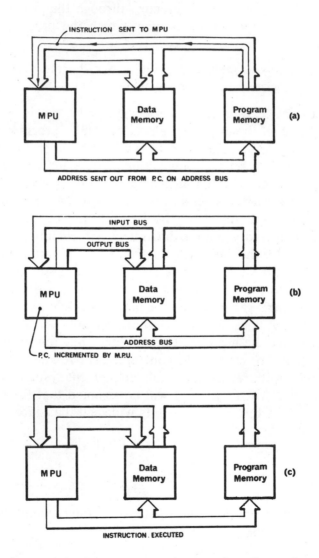

Figure 1-3. Basic instruction cycle of a micro-computer

The instruction cycle may be illustrated by considering the following simple program:

Step 0   Set the accumulator to zero
Step 1   Increment the accumulator
Step 2   Shift accumulator up one place

Assume that the program counter has been set to zero by some external mechanism. First of all, the program counter contents are sent out along the address bus (i.e., address 0 is on the address bus) as shown in Figure 1-3a. The program memory recognises address 0 as one of its own and it sends out the contents of address 0, which contains the instruction "Set accumulator to zero," onto the input bus. The MPU picks up the instruction and loads it into the instruction register. The contents of the program counter are then incremented as shown in Figure 1-3b. Then the instruction is executed, which in this case sets the accumulator to zero, and the state shown in Figure 1-3c is reached. This sequence of events completes Step 0 of the program and therefore constitutes the first instruction cycle. The system carries on to begin the next instruction cycle by sending out the contents of the program counter (now address 1) and the program memory replies by sending the instruction "Increment accumulator" to the instruction register. The program counter is incremented and so the cycle continues.

The instruction cycle given above is sufficient for the operation of a fairly simple microprocessor. However, since the input bus is only 8 bits wide, all instructions would have to be encoded into 8 bits. This only allows for 256 different instructions. This is inadequate for general use, and in order to overcome this problem, the concept of a multiple byte instruction is used. In a multiple byte instruction the complete instruction is encoded into a multiple of the byte size of the machine. For the 8-bit example used here, multiple byte instructions would be encoded into 16, 24, 32 bits, etc. The instruction is then split up into a group of bytes and written into the program as a series of program steps. For example, consider the three program steps:

Step 0   Increment accumulator
Step 1   Store the contents of the accumulator in data
         memory at address 1010101010101010
Step 2   Increment accumulator

In a particular MPU, the two instructions might be encoded as follows:

Increment accumulator   01001100

Store contents of   01110111 10101010 10101010
accumulator in data
memory at address
1010101010101010

In the program memory, the three program steps would then appear as:

Step 0   Address 0   01001100   = Increment
Step 1   Address 1   01110111 ⎤
         Address 2   10101010 ⎬ = Store
         Address 3   10101010 ⎦
Step 2   Address 4   01001100   = Increment

Note in particular how the "store" instruction has been split up into three 8-bit bytes.

In order to handle multiple byte instructions it is necessary to modify the instruction cycle a little so that all but the last byte of a multiple byte instruction are treated as instructions requiring no action. Thus the three program steps in the above example would create the interaction shown in Table 1-1.

Note how the 3-byte "store" instruction is transmitted from the program memory to the MPU in three separate instruction sub-cycles using the program counter to address each byte. The MPU recognises from the code of the first byte (Step 1, Cycle 1 that the instruction is a 3-byte instruction and waits until Cycle 3 before executing the full instruction. During the first two cycles it rebuilds the 24-bit instruction from the separate bytes. The time taken to execute two do-nothing commands is wasted. Thus some of the more sophisticated machines miss out the do-nothing commands so that the full instruction cycle for a 3-byte instruction

TABLE 1-1. MULTIPLE BYTE INSTRUCTION CYCLE EXAMPLE

Step 0
          Cycle
          {
          Send out p.c. contents (0) and fetch
            instruction
          Increment p.c.
          Execute instruction (increment acc.)

Step 1
          Send out p.c. contents (1) and fetch
            instruction

          Sub
          Cycle 1   Increment p.c.
                       Execute instruction (do-nothing)
                       Send out p.c. contents (2) and fetch
                         instruction
          Sub
          Cycle 2   Increment p.c.
                       Executive instruction (do-nothing)
                       Send out p.c. contents (3) and fetch
                         instruction
          Sub
          Cycle 3   Increment p.c.
                       Execute instruction (send contents of
                         acc.)

Step 2
          Cycle
          Send out p.c. contents (4) and fetch
            instruction
          Increment p.c.
          Execute instruction (increment acc.)

Instruction Cycle

would be:

    Send out p.c. contents and fetch instruction
    Increment program counter
    Send out p.c. contents and fetch instruction
    Increment program counter
    Send out p.c. contents and fetch instruction
    Increment program counter
    Execute instruction.

In practice, the system timing can become even more complicated because different instructions can take different times to execute. This topic will be covered in more detail in Chapters 2, 3 and 5.

Multiple byte instructions nearly always arise when the instruction contains two pieces of distinct formation:

(1)   The operation to be performed (e.g., store contents of accumulator)

(2)   An address relating to the data on which the operation is to be performed.

In the example given above, the first byte of the instruction specified the instruction to be performed and the last 2 bytes specified the address as follows:

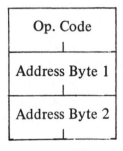

Generally, the first byte of the instruction is known as the "op-code" (short for operation code) and the other bytes are known quite naturally as the "address." So a multiple byte instruction may be depicted as follows:

Op. Code
Address Byte 1
Address Byte 2

Multiple byte instructions are not restricted to 3 bytes. Sometimes a 2-byte instruction is adequate, and occasionally 4 bytes are used.

INSTRUCTION TYPES

There are 4 basic types of instruction that are used in micro-processors; these are:

(1)   Arithmetic and logical instructions — such as add, subtract, shift, AND, OR, etc.

(2)   Instructions that work with memory. This can be data memory or program memory.

(3) Jump instructions. These make it possible to jump from one portion of a program to another.

(4) Input and output instructions. These make it possible for the system to communicate with the outside world.

It is quite common for a single instruction to have several of the properties listed, but it is convenient to separate them as above for explanatory purposes.

ARITHMETIC AND LOGICAL INSTRUCTIONS

These instructions operate upon data using the Arithmetic and Logical Unit (ALU) within the MPU. The ALU is a circuit which allows binary numbers to be added, subtracted, shifted, AND-ed, etc. For operations requiring two operands (e.g., addition), the accumulator is often the source for one of the operands and some other memory location or register is the source for the other. One or more flip-flops (often called flags) are associated with the ALU. These flip-flops relate to the overflow and underflow bits occuring during an ALU operation. Where only one flip-flop is used it may be considered as an extra bit added to the ALU, so that if an overflow takes place during an addition, then the flip-flop (often called carry-link flag) is set. In shift operations the operand can be shifted through the carry-link flag. It is important, when carrying out arithmetic and logical operations, to note whether the carry-link flag affects the outcome of the operation and also whether the carry-link flag is affected by the operation. This varies from processor to processor and is usually specified in the detailed explanation of each instruction.

Some MPU's have several flags (flip-flops) associated with the ALU. The various conditions that they can signify include:

Carry — from an arithmetic operation
Overflow — overflow as a result of an arithmetic operation
Link — used in shifting
Sign — usually the sign of the number in the accumulator
Parity — a parity bit relating to the number in the accumulator
Auxiliary — signifies a carry from bit 3 to bit 4 of the adder;

(or Half   — this is useful in BCD arithmetic operation
carry)

A typical set of arithmetic instructions would include some of the
following:

Add
Subtract
Shift left (i.e., multiply the number by 2)
Shift right (i.e., divide the number by 2)
AND
OR
Exclusive-OR
Complement
Clear accumulator (i.e., set accumulator to zero)
Increment
Decrement
Compare
Various instructions for manipulating the flags associated with
the ALU

MEMORY REFERENCE INSTRUCTIONS

A memory reference instruction is one which works with data that
is stored in either the program memory or the data memory. The
instruction "store accumulator contents at the address
1010101010101010," is a memory reference instruction because
it works with a binary number which is stored at the specified
address. Very often a memory reference instruction includes an
arithmetic or logical command. Examples of this are:

(1)   Add contents of specified memory address to accumulator

(2)   Subtract contents of specified memory address from accumu-
      lator

(3)   AND contents of specified memory address with accumu-
      lator

(4)   OR contents of specified memory address with accumulator

(5)   Exclusive-OR contents of specified memory address with
      accumulator

(6) Shift contents of specified memory address one place to the left

(7) Shift contents of specified memory address one place to the right

(8) Increment contents of specified memory address

(9) Decrement contents of specified memory address.

It should be noted that instructions 1 to 5 given above have two operands. One is held in the accumulator and the other is in the specified memory address. The final result is placed in the accumulator. However, instructions 6 to 9 begin with a single operand in a specified memory address. The operand is brought to the ALU in the microprocessor, and after performing the required task the result is placed back into the specified address. The accumulator is not affected by the operation. The above list is by no means exhaustive; some microprocessors do not have all the features given above, others have far more. Memory reference instructions are discussed in more detail in the next chapter.

JUMP INSTRUCTIONS

A jump instruction (sometimes called a branch instruction) is one which allows the microprocessor to move from one section of a program to another, without having to sequentially count through all the instructions before getting to the program segment of interest. Suppose a program contains three jobs, A, B and C, which the system has to do and these three jobs are written as three program segments one after the other as in Figure 1-4a. If for some reason it is required to reverse the order in which the jobs are carried out, this can be done by using jump instructions inserted as shown in Figure 1-4b. To carry out a jump instruction the program counter is loaded with the new value specified in the instruction. So in the example of Figure 1-4b, the program counter begins at zero, and the first instruction is a 3-byte jump instruction which commands a jump to program memory address number 43. The program then executes the instruction steps through instruction 44, 45, etc. until it reaches the instruction which is stored in program memory bytes 59, 60 and 61, which commands a jump to the instruction stored at memory location

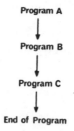

Figure 1-4a. Basic program layout

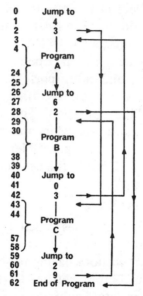

Figure 1-4b. Program flow with jump instructions

Figure 1-4. Illustration of action caused by jump instructions

29. This causes the program counter to be loaded with 29 and program B will then be carried out. Then program A is followed and the final jump is to the program end.

The type of jump instruction described above is known as an unconditional jump because the jump always takes place. A great deal of the power of a computer stems from its ability to make conditional jumps.

A typical conditional jump instruction would be the following:

"If condition X is true, then jump to a specified instruction number, but if X is not true, continue to the next instruction in sequence." The contents of a program counter, after a conditional jump instruction has been executed, can either be the next instruction in the sequence or a completely new instruction address specified by the conditional jump. An example might be:

If accumulator is zero, jump to address 1010101010101010 (if accumulator is not zero, go to the next instruction in sequence).

Normally the section in brackets is understood and it is not usually written as part of the instruction definition. Simple microprocessors have a limited range of jump instructions. These might be "Jump if carry-link = 1" and "Jump if accumulator is zero." Other units may have more jump conditions based on the condition of the ALU flags. An example of such a conditional jump would be "Jump if overflow is set." In some microprocessors the user defines the various jump instructions by means of hardware.

INPUT-OUTPUT INSTRUCTIONS

A microcomputer system is of little use by itself because there must be some way in which the user can put information in and get information out of the system. The communication channels which are used for input and output are usually called "ports," and all microprocessors have some instructions which make it possible to take information into the system via an input port and put information out via an output port.

Some microprocessors have special input and output instructions but others adapt normal memory reference instructions for the purpose. This subject is covered in Chapter 3.

SUMMARY OF INSTRUCTION TYPES

The above breakdown of instructions into 4 types is a nominal one because, in practice, many instructions fall into 2 or more of the categories (e.g., a jump instruction implies a memory reference operation). However, most manufacturers try to split up the instruction set in the above manner so as to aid the understanding of the set of instructions that a particular microprocessor will respond to. Inevitably a fifth category of "special instructions" tends to creep in, although with such a loose set of groupings to begin with, it is difficult to decide whether an instruction is special or normal. Some typical special instructions include things like "Stop," "Delay for n seconds," "Do-nothing," etc. The following chapters will cover the various instruction types in more detail.

EXAMPLE OF A MICROCOMPUTER PROGRAM

The example here illustrates how a typical microcomputer might add two numbers stored in memory locations 0000:0000:1000:0000 and 0000:0000:1000:0001 and place the result in memory location 0000:0000:1000:0010. A basic program is as follows:

Step 0 Clear accumulator

Step 1 Add contents of 0000:0000:1000:0000 to accumulator

Step 2 Add contents of 0000:0000:1000:0001 to accumulator

Step 3 Store accumulator contents at address 0000:0000:1000:0010

The instruction code for each of the three instructions is:

Clear accumulator

0 1 0 0 1 1 1 1

Add contents of memory to accumulator

1 0 1 1 1 0 0 1
High Address Byte
Low Address Byte

Store accumulator contents at specified address

1 0 1 1 0 1 1 1
High Address Byte
Low Address Byte

The program memory would then contain the following bit pattern:

Step Number	Program Memory Address	Contents
0	0	0 1 0 0 1 1 1 1
1	1	1 0 1 1 1 0 0 1
	2	0 0 0 0 0 0 0 0
	3	1 0 0 0 0 0 0 0
2	4	1 0 1 1 1 0 0 1
	5	0 0 0 0 0 0 0 0
	6	1 0 0 0 0 0 0 1
3	7	1 0 1 1 0 1 1 1
	8	0 0 0 0 0 0 0 0
	9	1 0 0 0 0 0 1 0

When the microcomputer begins the program, the program counter will be set to zero. The program counter contents will be sent out as an address (i.e., address 0) and the corresponding memory contents (01001111) will be returned to the instruction register. The MPU increments the program counter and then executes the instruction which is "Clear accumulator." The next instruction is a 3-byte instruction so that it will not be executed until the last byte has been received into the instruction register whereupon it will add the contents of the specified memory address to the accumulator.

This will be repeated for Step 2, but with a different address, and finally on Step 3 the contents of the accumulator will be sent to the specified address. Step 3 is also a 3-byte instruction, so execution of the instruction will not take place until the last byte has been received.

It should be noted that in order to encode four instructions into the program memory it has been necessary to use ten bytes of program memory. Different microprocessor designs try to reduce the program memory size for a given job by using variations on the basic instructions and architecture. Notice also that program step 2 begins at memory address 4, so that should it be necessary at any stage to jump to program step 2, the jump instruction should read "Jump to program memory location number 4."

USE OF THE INDEX REGISTER

For the above example it is possible to reduce the number of bytes of program memory required by using the index register. Note that the three data-memory addresses are consecutive; this is very common in computer programming. Therefore, if the index register is loaded with the address of the first memory location, there is no necessity to send the address to the MPU again.

Thus the instruction, "Add contents of memory location 0000:0000:1000:0000 to accumulator," becomes "Add contents of memory location specified by the index register." The second instruction can be encoded in one 8-bit byte because it does not specify a 16-bit address. Thus it becomes:

"Add contents of memory location specified by index register to accumulator"

1 0 0 0 0 1 1 0

Similarly, the store instruction can be written: "Store contents of accumulator at memory location specified by index register".

0 1 1 1 0 1 1 1

To assist in modifying the program, it is necessary to define two other instructions.

"Load index register with a specified 16-bit binary number"

0 0 1 0 0 0 0 1
High Address Byte
Low Address Byte

"Increment index register"

0 0 1 0 0 0 1 1

The program now becomes

Step 0   Clear accumulator

Step 1   Load index register with address 0000:0000:1000:0000

Step 2   Add contents of memory location specified by index register to accumulator

Step 3   Increment index register

Step 4   Add contents of memory location specified by index register to accumulator

Step 5   Increment index register

Step 6   Store contents of accumulator at address specified by index register.

The program memory would then contain the following bit pattern:

Step Number	Program Memory Address	Contents
0	0	0 1 0 0 1 1 1 1
1	1	0 0 1 0 0 0 0 1
	2	0 0 0 0 0 0 0 0
	3	1 0 0 0 0 0 0 0
2	4	1 0 0 0 0 1 1 0
3	5	0 0 1 0 0 0 1 1
4	6	1 0 0 0 0 1 1 0
5	7	0 0 1 0 0 0 1 1
6	8	0 1 1 1 0 1 1 1

The necessary data memory addresses are held in the index register and, because the required addresses are consecutive, the next address can be created by incrementing the index register. This saves time and storage because it is not necessary to send a new address each time a memory reference instruction is used. For the example used here the saving is small (just one memory byte), but computer programs often require a sequential scan through large blocks of data and then the saving in the program memory size can be quite significant.

INSTRUCTION NOTATION METHODS

Even with the simple examples used already, there has been some textual difficulty in writing the programs. The description of each instruction is rather long and writing of binary numbers is tedious and prone to error. Therefore, it is convenient to adopt shorthand schemes to assist in presenting the information in a precise and concise manner. As an example consider the instruction:

"Add contents of memory location 0000:0000:1000:0001 to the accumulator."

This can be shortened to:

ADA   [0081]

ADA is a mnemonic for "Add to accumulator." The square brackets signify "the contents of the enclosed address," and 0081 is the address written in hexadecimal format.

Each microprocessor has its own unique set of instructions and its own set of mnemonics. There is no international standardisation. Manufacturers usually provide detailed lists of the mnemonics, their formats and their meanings.

Fortunately, there are relatively few shorthand methods of writing binary numbers and there is a definite trend towards the hexadecimal method. With this method the binary number is split into blocks of 4 bits and then each block is written down as its equivalent decimal number. For binary numbers in the range 1010 (ten) to 1111 (fifteen), the first few letters of the alphabet are used. The complete conversion table is as follows:

TABLE 1-2. BINARY TO HEXADECIMAL CONVERSION TABLE

0000	0	1000	8
0001	1	1001	9
0010	2	1010	A
0011	3	1011	B
0100	4	1100	C
0101	5	1101	D
0110	6	1110	E
0111	7	1111	F

An alternative method is to split the binary number into blocks of 3 bits and then write down the equivalent decimal number. Since the largest number using 3 bits is 7, this is known as the octal representation.

e.g. 1010101010101010 becomes 1010:1010:1010:1010 =

AAAA in hexadecimal

and becomes 1:010:101:010:101:010 =

125252 in octal code.

It should be understood that the various mnemonics and number codes are purely to assist the user in writing and understanding the program. In the program memory all instructions are stored as binary numbers. Also note that there are two shorthand methods of writing the instruction. The first is a letter-type mnemonic giving the action of the instruction (e.g., ADA), and the second method is the hexadecimal code for the binary form of the instruction.

e.g., ADA   [0081] has the binary code

1011:1001 ← Op. code

0000:0000⎫
          ⎬ Address
1000:0001⎭

which may be written   B9
                        00
                        81   in hexadecimal code.

Programs which are written either in pure binary code or in hexadecimal (or octal code) are generally referred to as being written in "machine code." Programs written using alphabetic mnemonics are usually called "assembly language programs."

SUMMARY

The function of this chapter has been to explain some of the more fundamental microprocessor principles. It should be remembered that no two microprocessors are the same, and the examples given above are intended purely to illustrate certain points. They do not refer to any particular system and in practice are subject to various refinements.

Memory Addressing

Chapter 2

INTRODUCTION

In a microcomputer system, the microprocessor serves to manipulate the binary information which is stored in memory. The ease and speed with which the microprocessor can gain access to any particular word stored in the memory will determine the speed at which a particular program can be executed, and also the size of the program. It follows that the structure and execution time of the various instructions, which require interaction with memory, have great bearing on the overall size and efficiency of the complete microcomputer system, and are therefore of vital importance. A microprocessor with a powerful "instruction set" yields a design which will use the minimum number of memory elements, and therefore cost less. In practice, the memory is a much larger portion of a complete system than the microprocessor itself, and in even the smallest systems there are usually two memory elements (one for program and one for data) to one microprocessor, and it is not unusual to find 30 or more memory packages supporting one microprocessor. Clearly, the microprocessor system designer needs to study the instruction set very carefully to ensure that it gives the smallest program for the particular application under consideration. However, there is no single criterion which covers all jobs, and each situation must be assessed on its own merits.

Instructions which work with information stored in memory are usually known as "memory reference instructions," and they fall into two broad categories; those which address data, and those which address the program memory. A data reference instruction might be "Store contents of accumulator at location ABCD," and a jump instruction is one type of instruction which causes interaction with the program memory. Generally speaking, once a program has been loaded into a microcomputer system it does not modify itself: this means that it is not normal to write information into the program memory during program run time and therefore most program memory reference instructions are of the type "Read contents of program memory location ABCD." There are two reasons for this restriction on the program memory: firstly, it is poor programming practice to have a program which modifies itself because it makes system crashes more likely, and secondly, program memory is often the "read only" type in which write operations are impossible.

ARITHMETIC AND LOGICAL OPERATIONS

There is a wide range of arithmetic and logical instructions that can be found in microprocessors. Some processors have only an elementary set such as add, subtract and shift; others include instructions such as exclusive-OR, AND, compare, etc. In general, most microprocessors carry out binary arithmetic using two's complement number representation, and one remarkable feature of nearly all units is that they include facilities for operations on BCD numbers as well as on binary numbers. This is something that many of the larger computers do not have.

The minimum set of arithmetic and logical instructions would probably be:

(1) Add
(2) Subtract
(3) Shift left through carry-link flag
(4) Shift right through carry-link flag
(5) Clear carry-link flag
(6) Clear accumulator
(7) Complement accumulator
(8) Complement carry.

Using this basic set of instructions it would be possible to build up other more sophisticated operations such as AND, OR, exclusive-OR, etc. Note in particular that instructions 1 and 2

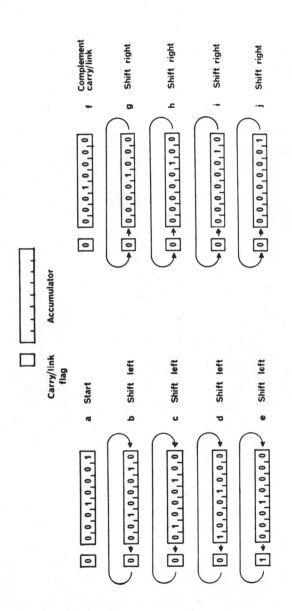

Figure 2-1. Complementing bit 4 by rotating through carry/link flag

above require two operands, with one most probably held in the accumulator and the other held in memory, whereas the remainder of the instructions operate on information already held within the microprocessor. This means that the instruction cycle for items 3 to 8 will be the simple procedure:

(a)　Send out p.c. contents and fetch instruction
(b)　Increment p.c.
(c)　Execute the instruction.

But the instruction cycle for items 1 and 2 will be more complex. If the instruction is "Add the contents of the address specified by the index register to the accumulator," then the instruction cycle would be:

(a)　Send out p.c. contents and fetch instruction
(b)　Increment p.c.
(c)　Send out index register contents as an address and fetch data to microprocessor
(d)　Add accumulator and the data just fetched.

A memory reference instruction is implied by the add instruction because one of the operands is held in memory. In this particular case the appropriate address is specified by the index register, but there are many ways of specifying a particular data address and these will be the subject of much of this chapter.

The carry-link flag can in many cases be considered as a 1-bit extension of the accumulator register. By rotating the accumulator through the carry-link flag and using those instructions which set, clear and complement the carry-link flag, it is possible to gain access to and modify any single bit within the accumulator. Clearly this can be quite a slow process when, for example, it is required to complement bit 4 in an 8-bit accumulator. Such a program would involve 4 shifts left, complement carry-link, and 4 shifts right — a total of 9 instructions which is quite wasteful in program memory storage space (see Figure 2-1). A much neater operation would be to exclusive-OR the contents of the accumulator with 00010000. This would achieve the same result and probably use only 2 bytes of program storage. The more sophisticated arithmetic and logical instructions can therefore save quite a lot of program storage space. Instructions in this category include:

Increment
Decrement
AND
OR
Exclusive-OR
Compare
Logical and Arithmetic shifts.
(A logical shift is one in which the bit shifted in is determined by the state of the carry flag, whereas for an arithmetic shift, the bit shifted in is determined by the number convention in use — usually two's complement.)

The ability to operate with numbers in BCD format is an important feature because microprocessors are usually quite close to the man-machine interface, and it is often faster and more convenient to work with BCD numbers throughout than do conversions to and from binary. There are several levels of "BCD ability," ranging from simple instructions which convert the result of a BCD addition back into BCD right up to processors which can operate throughout in either a BCD or two's complement binary mode. For example, consider the case where 28 is added to 39, both numbers being represented in 8-bit BCD format. The result after a straightforward binary addition is shown below:

$$
\begin{array}{r}
0010\,{:}\,1000 \\
0011\,{:}\,1001 \\
\hline
0110\,{:}\,0001 \\
\end{array}
$$

In order to restore the number to its true BCD result, the microprocessor has to execute a special instruction which converts the number in the accumulator back into BCD format — this instruction is usually called "decimal adjust accumulator." The decimal adjust accumulator instruction (usual mnemonic DAA) uses the information that a carry took place from the low order BCD character to the high order character to restore the least significant digit to its correct value of 0111. So for each BCD addition using the process described above the programmer has to write two instructions:

(1) Add
(2) Decimal adjust accumulator.

Carry flag before DAA	Upper half-byte	Half carry before DAA	Lower half-byte	Number added to Acc.	Carry flag after DAA
0	0 to 9	0	0 to 9	00	0
0	0 to 8	0	A to F	06	0
0	0 to 9	1	0 to 3	06	0
0	A to F	0	0 to 9	60	1
0	9 to F	0	A to F	66	1
0	A to F	1	0 to 3	66	1
1	0 to 2	0	0 to 9	60	1
1	0 to 2	0	A to F	66	1
1	0 to 3	1	0 to 3	66	1

Figure 2-2. DAA (decimal adjust accumulator) algorithm for an 8-bit microprocessor

Machines with separate binary and BCD addition instructions do not require the decimal adjust accumulator instruction and this gives a saving in program size. Figure 2-2 gives the full algorithm which the DAA instruction uses: it should be noted that it relies on the carry and half-carry flags for its operation. These are explained below.

ARITHMETIC FLAGS

The accumulator of a microprocessor usually has a number of flags (or flip-flops) associated with it. These flags signify that certain events have taken place and the operation of some instructions depends upon the state of these flags. The flags are often referred to as "status flags" and the binary word made up of their various states is called the "status word." The set of flags may be considered to be an additional register within the MPU called the "status register."

The status flags vary from processor to processor. The most fundamental flags are:

(a)   Carry-link flag
(b)   Half-carry flag (this is necessary for the DAA instruction).

The carry-link flag is set if an arithmetic operation yields a carry.

Alternatively it may be used with shift operations as described above. The half-carry flag is set if a carry propagates from the 4 least significant bits to the 4 most significant bits in the course of an arithmetic operation. Its main function is to aid the operation of the "decimal adjust accumulator" instruction, but it can be used for other purposes.

Other flags can include a parity flag, a sign flag, a zero flag relating to the number in the accumulator, and also an overflow flag denoting an overflow as the result of an arithmetic operation. It is important to recognise the difference between an overflow and a carry. The carry flag is set when an arithmetic operation results in a carry; the overflow flag is only set when an arithmetic operation yields a true arithmetic overflow. For example, +5 minus +3 in two's complement gives a carry-out of the high order end. However, the result +2 is still within the number range of the machine so the overflow is not set. Conversely, minus 100 plus minus 64 on an 8-bit machine gives a carry-out plus an overflow because the result is a positive 8-bit number even though the result should be negative in true arithmetic terms.

Machines with an interrupt system also have an interrupt mask flag which is usually included as part of the status register. This particular flag is related to input-output operations and is not directly affected by arithmetic operations (see Chapter 3).

MEMORY REFERENCE INSTRUCTIONS – CLASSICAL APPROACH

DIRECT, INDIRECT AND IMMEDIATE ADDRESSING

A memory reference instruction is one which refers to memory in order to obtain an operand. The instruction "Add contents of memory address ABCD to accumulator" is an example of a memory reference instruction. In an 8-bit microprocessor this instruction would probably have the structure as follows:

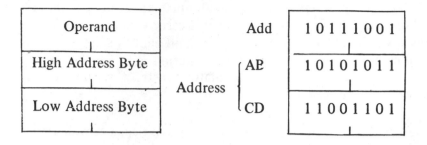

The type of instruction given here, where the address of the relevant data is contained explicity within the instruction, is known as direct addressing. This mode of addressing has severe limitations because, every time a data address is used, it has to be included in the instruction. For example, if it is required to find the average of four numbers stored in addresses ABCA, ABCB, ABCC and ABCD (hexadecimal notation), then the program using direct addressing would be:

Clear Accumulator
Add [ABCA]
Add [ABCD]
Add [ABCC]
Add [ABCD]
Shift Right
Shift Right

This program would leave the average value in the accumulator.

In Chapter 1 it was shown how it is possible to reduce the amount of program storage space by utilising the fact that the numbers are stored in consecutive locations. The index register was used to "point" to each data item and the instruction simply specified that the relevant data address was to be found in the index register. This type of instruction, where the actual data address is not explicit in the instruction but is held in some other location, is known as indirect addressing. In its most general form the pointer location can be any memory address and it can point to any other location.

In the averaging example used above, it would be possible to use memory location ABCE as the address pointer by using the instruction "Add @ [ABCE]." The @ sign denotes that indirect addressing is to be used. If it is assumed that when the program begins memory location ABCE holds the value ABCA, then the program using indirect addressing will be:

Clear Accumulator
Add @ [ABCE]
Increment [ABCE]
Add @ [ABCE]
Increment [ABCE]
Add @ [ABCE]
Increment [ABCE]
Add @ [ABCE]
Shift Right
Shift Right

Instead of using the index register to point to the consecutive memory addresses, the program has used memory location ABCE to store the pointer. As it stands, the program would in fact use more program memory space with indirect addressing than it would with direct addressing. However, as will be shown later, use may be made of the fact that the instruction sequence "Add @ [ABCE]" followed by "Increment [ABCE]" occurs three times.

The binary op-code for the instruction "Add @ [ABCE]" would not be the same as that for "Add [ABCE]"; it would most likely differ by 1 bit. The two instruction codes might be as shown below:

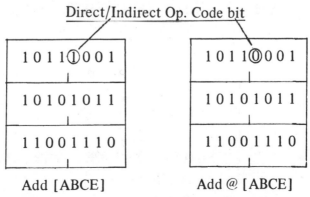

Direct/Indirect Op. Code bit

| Add [ABCE] | Add @ [ABCE] |

As indicated below, the instruction cycle for direct addressing is shorter than that for indirect addressing: this will mean that the cycle time for direct addressing is less than that for indirect addressing. The instruction cycle for direct addressing is:

Send out p.c. contents and fetch op-code
Increment p.c.
Send out p.c. contents and fetch high order address bytes
Increment p.c.
Send out p.c. contents and fetch low order address bytes
Increment p.c.
Send out data address, fetch data and execute instruction.

The instruction cycle for indirect addressing is:

Send out p.c. contents and fetch op-code
Increment p.c.
Send out p.c. contents and fetch high order pointer address bytes
Increment p.c.
Send out p.c. contents and fetch low order pointer address bytes
Increment p.c.
Send out pointer address and fetch data address
Send out data address, fetch data and execute instruction.

Apart from direct and indirect addressing, there is one other fundamental addressing mode known as immediate addressing. In immediate addressing the operand is contained within the instruction itself; a typical immediate addressing instruction might be "Add the constant ABCE (hexadecimal notation) to the accumulator." The binary instruction format would be

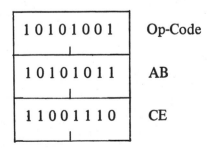

and a typical mnemonic would be "Add # ABCE." The symbol

# denotes immediate addressing. Since the relevant data is contained in the instruction itself, immediate addressing does not need to reference the data memory. Immediate addressing is useful where it is required to introduce constants into a program. Setting up address ABCE to contain ABCA for the start of the indirect addressing program above would probably be done using immediate addressing as follows:

Clear accumulator
Add # ABCA
Store [ABCE]

The value ABCA is added to the accumulator and then the contents of the accumulator are stored at address ABCE. In the above example the "store" instruction provides another example of direct addressing; it is of course possible to have store instructions which use indirect addressing.

REFINEMENTS TO MEMORY ADDRESSING MODES

Direct and indirect addressing can be further enhanced by including additional features such as autoincrement, autodecrement and indexed addressing. These refinements are additional to the basic addressing modes so that it is possible to have, for example, an indirect, autoincrement addressing mode. In the average program using indirect addressing, the sequence of instructions

Add @ [ABCE]
Increment [ABCE]

occurred several times. Some processors can combine these two instructions into one so that a single instruction adds the contents of the address specified by the address stored at location ABCE, and also automatically increments the contents of location ABCE. The automatic incrementing feature is known as autoincrement and a similar facility for decrementing is known as autodecrement. Automatic incrementing and decrementing are particularly useful where the program works with large quantities of data which are stored in consecutive memory locations. This occurs in matrix operations. Another refinement which is particularly useful in complicated programs is indexed addressing. With indexed addressing the correct data address is calculated by adding an offset value to a specified address. Usually, the offset is stored in the index register and the specified address can be obtained by direct or indirect addressing. For example, if the index register contains 0005 and the instruction is "Add [0A00] indexed," then the correct data address would be obtained by adding 0A00 to 0005 to give the correct address at 0A05. It is possible to have an indexed autoincrement indirect addressing mode, where the correct address is obtained by adding the index register to the indirectly specified address and then the index register is automatically incremented: sometimes the indirect address is incremented rather than the index register.

RELATIVE ADDRESSING

Relative addressing is very similar to indexed addressing in that the correct address is calculated by adding an offset to some base address. The instruction contains the offset value and the program counter usually provides the base address. This relationship with the program counter means that relative addressing is often used in connection with jump instructions. Relative addressing is also important when writing programs which may be subsequently moved to another portion of the program memory.

CLASSICAL STRUCTURE OF THE OP-CODE FOR MEMORY REFERENCE INSTRUCTIONS

Very often the binary op-code for memory reference instructions is built up according to a neat logical pattern. This makes it much easier to write assembler programs. (An assembler is a computer program, which reads a program written in mnemonics and converts it into a program written in binary or hexadecimal characters.)

Figure 2-3 shows a possible structure for the op-code of an 8-bit microprocessor. This op-code would of course occur together with the appropriate address bytes.

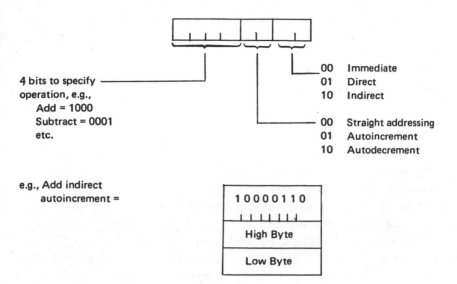

Figure 2-3 Possible op-code structure

MEMORY REFERENCE INSTRUCTIONS FOR MICROPROCESSORS

Microprocessors try to meet two criteria which often conflict; the need for a powerful instruction set and the requirement for instructions which use the minimum amount of program storage. In order to meet these goals various methods are used to reduce the number of bytes in a particular instruction. Usually this entails reducing the addressing capability of the memory reference instructions whilst retaining the essential character of the classical instruction. Some of the more common approaches are given below. It should be remembered that reducing the number of bytes in an instruction also reduces the cycle time of an instruction and therefore speeds up the program.

REGISTER ADDRESSING

The 3-byte indirect addressing instruction of the form

| Op-Code |
| High Address Byte |
| Low Address Byte |

contains the ability to use any memory location as a pointer to the appropriate data address. In practice, this complete flexibility is usually not required and it is adequate to have only one or two "address pointers." By doing this it is possible to reduce the instruction from a three-byte instruction to a single-byte instruction where the actual address pointer is specified within the op-code. Most microprocessors have at least one register within the MPU which can be used as an address pointer and this is usually the index register. The example in Chapter 1 shows how it is possible to achieve a form of indirect addressing using the index register. Some MPU's have only one index register whereas others have several within the processor.

Register addressing is used as a standard approach for computers much larger than microprocessors because of the tremendous saving in program storage and the resultant improvement in instruction cycle time.

PAGING

Register addressing gives a considerable improvement for indirect addressing operations, but it is not applicable to direct addressing. One way of speeding up direct addressing operations is to use paging. With paging, the high address byte is stored within the microprocessor in some register and only the low address byte is specified by the direct addressing instruction. This approach makes use of the fact that most of the addresses which the microprocessor is working with at any one time are fairly close to each other, and therefore will have the same high order address byte. The splitting up of the memory address into a high order byte and a low order byte is akin to the division of a book into a series of pages, and hence the term paging.

The efficient use of paging normally requires at least one extra register in the MPU to specify the page number and also some additional instructions which make it possible to change page numbers whenever necessary. It also entails taking extra care when programming to make sure that page boundaries are not crossed inadvertently. An alternative to having an extra register for storing the page number is to restrict direct addressing to a single page, say page 0, so that when a direct addressing instruction is received by the MPU, it knows that the high order bits are all logical zero. This method also saves having extra instructions for changing page numbers.

Paging is a very powerful tool and has been applied in many different ways. For example, it can be used in conjunction with the program counter to reduce the number of bytes in a jump instruction. Broadly speaking, paging finds greatest application in 4- and 8-bit microprocessors and where the number of available pins on a microprocessor is severely restricted.

ON-CHIP REGISTER ADDRESSING

Some microprocessors have several additional general purpose registers within the MPU as shown in Figure 2-4. Usually special instructions are provided so that these registers can be directly addressed with a single-byte instruction. The term "inherent" addressing has been applied to this type of operation because the

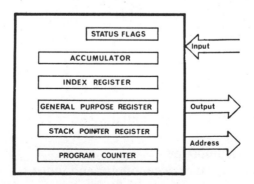

Figure 2-4. Microprocessor with multiple internal registers

data address is inherent in the single-byte op-code. These general purpose registers may be used for data storage or as address pointers in the same way as the index register is used.

BUILDING UP SOPHISTICATED MEMORY REFERENCE INSTRUCTIONS

Usually a microprocessor does not have all the addressing modes mentioned above, and in assessing a microprocessor it is worthwhile checking how many bytes of program are required to implement all the classical memory reference instructions. For example, quite a few microprocessors do not have any direct addressing facilities and a direct addressing instruction might have to be built up as follows:

Load the index register with the required address (3 bytes)
Add contents of address specified by index register to accumulator (1 byte).

Indirect addressing with autoincrement can be very difficult if there are no facilities for incrementing the on-chip registers. In this case, incrementing would have to be done using the accumulator so that the contents of the accumulator would have to be temporarily stored whilst the accumulator is used. In such a case the two instructions

Add contents of memory location specified by index register to accumulator (1 byte)
Increment index register (1 byte)

might have to be written

Add contents of location specified by index register to accumulator	(1 byte)
Exchange contents of accumulator and index register	(1 byte)
Increment accumulator	(1 byte)
Exchange contents of accumulator and index register	(1 byte)
Total	4 bytes.

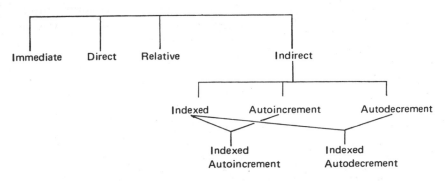

Figure 2-5. Fundamental addressing modes

It is unlikely that a microprocessor has ever been designed with such a restrictive set of instructions, but the above example does serve to illustrate the problems that can easily arise. Figure 2-5 gives a table of the various classical addressing modes for easy reference.

JUMP AND CONDITIONAL JUMP INSTRUCTIONS

Jump instructions are ones which can cause the program counter to be loaded with a new value instead of allowing it to continue through the program. This is an important point because the manner and the type of instructions which can change the program counter vary widely. The second, and equally important feature of jump instructions, is that "conditional jump" instructions give the program the ability to make decisions. An example of this might be "Jump to specified address if accumulator is zero, otherwise continue with normal program flow." Such an instruction would test the contents of the accumulator to see if it is zero. If it is, the program counter would be loaded with the address specified in the instruction; if the accumulator was not zero, the program counter contents would remain untouched and the program would continue in a straight numerical sequence. To illustrate this, consider the example in this chapter which finds the average of four numbers stored in locations ABCA, ABCB, ABCC, and ABCD. Assume that the microprocessor which is to be used has the internal register structure shown in Figure 2-4. Note in particular that a general purpose register (GPR) has been added to the fundamental architecture used so far. This general purpose register will be used for counting the number of times the program executes the add instruction. The averaging program now becomes:

Instruction No.	Program memory store
(1) Load immediate index register with ABCA	3 bytes
(2) Load immediate GPR with 0004	3 bytes
(3) Clear accumulator	1 byte
(4) Add contents of location specified by index register	1 byte
(5) Increment index register	1 byte
(6) Decrement GPR	1 byte
(7) If GPR ≠ zero jump back to add instruction	3 bytes
(8) Shift right	1 byte
(9) Shift right	1 byte
Total	15 bytes.

Figure 2-6 shows the corresponding program flow chart.

The conditional jump instruction "If GPR does not equal zero, jump back to add instruction" provides the program with the ability to make the elementary decision on whether to go around the loop once more, or whether to finish the addition. In practice the conditional jump contains an address to which the jump should take place rather than the indefinite statement "Jump to add instruction." The final program pattern in program memory would be as shown in Figure 2-7, where the jump instruction now specifies a jump to program memory location 0007. If the general purpose register is not equal to zero, the program counter will be loaded with the value 0007 and its current contents 000D will be lost.

If the general-purpose register had not been included, it would have been much more difficult to write the program, because the results of the addition and the contents of the loop counter would have had to be continually exchanged and moved around to utilise the accumulator, and any advantage in using the addition

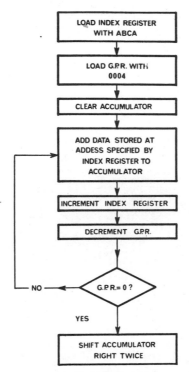

Figure 2-6. Program flow-chart for averaging example

loop approach would have been lost. For this reason all micro-processors include at least one general-purpose register for loop counting and other functions. Another point to note from the above example is that great use is made of the indirect addressing approach using the index register. The ability to dynamically create a new address from existing information within the program is essential for most applications.

The address to which the program jump takes place does not have to be explicit in the program as it was above. The particular type of jump used above was a version of a conditional immediate addressing instruction: "If condition is satisfied, load program counter with data which is contained in this instruction." In just the same way it is possible to use direct and indirect addressing to specify the value with which the program counter must be loaded.

Instruction No.	Program memory contents	Program memory address (hex.)
	Load IR immediate	0000
1	A B	0001
	C A	0002
	Load GPR immediate	0003
2	0 0	0004
	0 4	0005
3	Clear accumulator	0006
4	Add @ IR	0007
5	Increment IR	0008
6	Decrement GPR	0009
	If GPR ≠ 0 Jump	000A
7	0 0	000B
	0 7	000C
8	Shift right	000D
9	Shift right	000E

Figure 2-7. Program memory contents for averaging program

For example, the instruction "If condition is satisfied load program counter with the contents of address specified by the index register" is an indirect addressing jump instruction. These types of jumps add great power to the instruction set, and furthermore can reduce the number of bytes in an instruction. A jump instruction with immediate or direct addressing requires three bytes of memory, whereas an instruction with indirect addressing using the index register can be accommodated in a single program byte.

In some processors the program counter, the index register, the general-purpose register(s) and the accumulator are all regarded as general-purpose registers for some operations. Therefore the instruction "Load immediate ABCD to register A" could have quite different effects depending on what function register A is used for. For example, if the registers are lettered as follows,

A – Accumulator
B – Index register
C – General purpose register
D – Program counter

then "Load immediate ABCD to register A" will load the accumulator with value ABCD, but "Load immediate ABCD to register D" would cause a program jump to the program location ABCD. This approach can give the suprising impression that at first glance some microprocessors appear to have no specific jump instructions.

CONDITIONAL JUMP INSTRUCTIONS

The unconditional jump causes a jump to another section of program without having to test for any particular condition existing. By comparison the conditional jump (sometimes called a conditional branch instruction) requires that a ·condition be satisfied before the jump can take place, and it is this condition that gives the power of decision.

Conditional jumps usually base their decisions on the condition of the various arithmetic flags. The following is a list of some of the conditions that are available:

Carry-link flag set	Carry-link flag not set
Half-carry flag set	Half-carry flag not set
Accumulator zero	Accumulator not zero
Overflow flag set	Overflow flag not set
Parity flag set	Parity flag not set
Accumulator positive	Accumulator negative.

It is normal for the binary op-code of a conditional jump instruction to have an ordered structure such as that shown below.

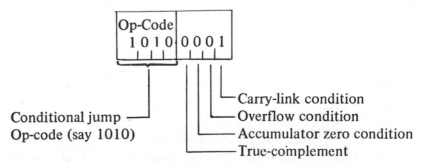

For example, "Jump to ABCD if carry-link set," would be:

```
1 0 1 0 0 0 0 1
1 0 1 0 1 0 1 1
1 1 0 0 1 1 0 1
```

The true-complement-bit gives the instruction the power to negate the condition so that the instruction "Jump to 0007 if accumulator not zero," would become:

```
1 0 1 0 1 1 0 0
0 0 0 0 0 0 0 0
0 0 0 0 0 1 1 1
```

The "1" in the true-complement-bit signifies that the complement of the condition should be satisfied, which in this case is a zero condition in the accumulator. Another common feature is the power to AND conditions together. For example, the instruction "Jump to ABBA if accumulator is zero AND carry-link is set" would become:

```
1 0 1 0 0 1 0 1
1 0 1 0 1 0 1 1
1 0 1 1 1 0 1 0
```

REDUCING THE NUMBER OF BYTES IN A JUMP INSTRUCTION

In previous sections various methods were discussed for reducing the number of bytes in memory reference instructions. The methods of indirect register addressing and paging are applicable to jump instructions. Several forms of paging can be used with jump instructions: the most simple form is where the high order program counter address bytes remain unchanged by the jump instruction, and only the low order bytes are loaded from the jump instruction. This means that it is only possible to jump within a program page but this is often adequate. An alternative approach is to add some number to the program counter. This number can either be specified in the jump instruction (i.e., immediate addressing) or in a register. The term "relative addressing" (see section RELATIVE ADDRESSING) is used to describe this operation since the jump is by some displacement relative to the program counter.

In microprocessors using 8-bit instruction bytes, and a 16-bit address, relative addressing makes it possible to reduce a jump instruction from three bytes to two bytes.

One particular type of instruction which can achieve a conditional jump with only a single instruction byte is the skip instruction which has the form "If condition XYZ is satisfied then skip the next n instructions." This makes it possible for the program to jump over the n instructions without executing them. The skip instruction has not been used much in microprocessors to date although some of the early devices used it to reduce the amount of program bytes in loop-counting applications.

SUBROUTINES

The instruction "Jump to subroutine" is much the same as a normal jump instruction. However, when a subroutine jump takes place, the program counter contents are not lost, but are temporarily stored in some special location where they can be recovered for later use. Subroutine jumps can be conditional or unconditional. A subroutine is used where a section of program such as multiplication is repeated several times during the course of the overall task. To write the same program each time it is needed is very wasteful in program storage space. The subroutine jump provides a method of holding the subroutine (e.g., multiply) in program memory only once. Each time the program is required, the main program jumps to the subroutine, and once the sub-task

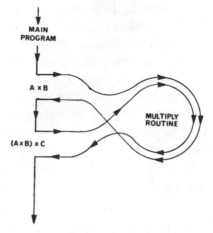

Figure 2-8a.

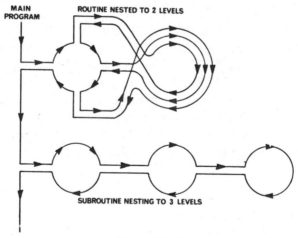

Figure 2-8b.

Figure 2-8. Illustrations of program flow using subroutines

is completed, control is returned to the program at the point it left off. Figure 2-8a shows schematically how a subroutine would be used in the case of a program to multiply three numbers together. Often it is required to "nest" subroutines so that one subroutine can call another subroutine. For example, an integration subroutine might call a division subroutine, and this situation of nested subroutines is schematically shown in Figure 2-8b. The problem in these circumstances is how to store the program counter contents, so that each time a return from subroutine is made the program counter is reloaded with the correct value.

In order to overcome this difficulty the concept of a subroutine "stack" is usually used. Each time a jump to subroutine is made, the current program counter contents are loaded onto a stack in the same way as one would stack plates. The value loaded onto the stack is always placed at the top of the stack. When a return from subroutine is made, the value stored at the top of the stack is loaded back into the program counter. These two operations are usually called "Push" for loading onto the stack, and "Pop" for taking values from off the stack. A "Jump to subroutine" instruction would have the following basic instruction cycle:

Send out p.c. contents and fetch instruction
Increment p.c.
Load p.c. contents onto stack
Load p.c. with address of subroutine specified in instruction.

Stacks can be implemented in two basic ways. One is to use a shift-register (sometimes called "Pushdown stack") where a "Push" corresponds to shifting the register one direction and a "Pop" corresponds to shifting in the opposite direction. The other method is to use a random access memory plus a stack pointer. The stack pointer is a register within the MPU which is specifically reserved for the purpose of keeping track of the next memory location available on the stack. A "Jump to subroutine" instruction with a microprocessor which uses a stack pointer has the instruction cycle:

Send out p.c. contents and fetch instruction
Increment p.c.
Load p.c. contents at memory location specified by stack pointer register
Increment stack pointer
Load p.c. with start address of subroutine.

The corresponding "Return from subroutine" would have the following instruction cycle:

Send out p.c. contents and fetch instruction
Decrement stack pointer
Load p.c. from address specified by stack pointer.

The shift register type of stack has been chiefly used where the stack is an integral part of the microprocessor chip, but it has the severe limitation that the number of stages in the "shift register" are limited, and therefore the number of levels to which sub-routines can be nested are limited. With the stack-pointer approach, the stack can be any size the system designer chooses since the stack is usually exterior to the processor and can be part of the same memory as the data storage memory.

Push and Pop instructions can be quite powerful in their own right, particularly if instructions provide for Pushing and Popping other registers, apart from the program counter, onto the stack. Furthermore, in some cases it is desirable to store not only the p.c. contents on the stack when a jump to subroutine occurs, but also the contents of all the other registers. This is particularly true in the case of real-time interrupts (see Chapter 3) and re-entrant sub-routines. A re-entrant subroutine is one which can be interrupted by one program and then called by another program. Once the second call has been completed, the interrupted subroutine is restarted where it left off. Since a subroutine usually changes the contents of the various registers, it is necessary to save all register contents before starting another run of the same subroutine. The Push and Pop instructions for various registers give this ability.

In addition to the stack architectures described above, several other methods have been used to save the program counter contents when jumping to a subroutine. One approach is to use multiple program counters and simply switch from one program counter to another when a subroutine call is made: this method gives a very fast change over. Another method is to exchange the program counter contents with the contents of a general-purpose register. Where limited subroutine nesting is required this tech-nique is adequate, but subroutine nesting to several levels usually has to be done by means of software and this slows down the overall program flow.

MULTIPLE ADDRESS MACHINES

To date the text has concentrated on machines where each addressing instruction specified one data address: where two operands are required, as in an add instruction, the second operand is provided by the accumulator. More general instructions would be of the type:

(i)   Add contents of address A to contents of address B and place results at address C

or

(ii)   Add contents of address A to contents of address B and place results at address B.

Type (i) is for a 3-address machine and is only found in very large computers. Type (ii) is for a 2-address machine. Instructions like this are much more powerful than those for single-address machines discussed so far, but in order to specify more than one address more bits are needed in the instruction, and so the amount of program storage for each instruction increases. Of course the addresses do not have to be directly addressed and, in fact, indirect addressing via registers is often preferable. This gives a significant reduction in instruction size and complexity. A machine operating in the 2-address mode might typically have 8 general-purpose registers. An add instruction could take the form:

Add contents of address specified by register 1 to contents of address specified by register 2 and place result at address specified by register 2 and increment register 1.

Such an instruction uses indirect addressing via registers for both addresses with autoincrement applied to register 1.

Multiple-address machines are of particular advantage in applications that process large amounts of data: the advantage is less pronounced where the emphasis is on real-time data handling.

SUMMARY

This chapter has attempted to describe the types of instruction usually used with microprocessors. Because microprocessors are small machines with a restricted number of pin connections, certain economies have to be made and various techniques are employed so as to obtain maximum computing power within these constraints. Inevitably different microprocessors use different instructions and architectures to achieve their goal. A micro-processor intended for "number crunching" applications such as intelligent calculators, would place emphasis on sophisticated addressing modes, whereas a device intended for, say, domestic control purposes, like an automatic washing machine, would be more concerned with obtaining a low-cost product with easy input-output facilities. The microprocessor designer chooses the best compromise compatible with his terms of reference, and consequently, no two microprocessors have identical instruction sets.

Input-Output Operations

Chapter 3

INTRODUCTION

To perform any useful task, the microcomputer must interact with the outside world. The input-output (I/O) devices or peripherals provide the necessary data communications link between the microprocessor and its environment. Typically, information is accepted from the input devices, it is processed and the results of the data processing are then sent to one or more output devices. In a microcomputer system, the input-output operations are particularly important since, in the majority of applications, the microprocessor spends the greatest part of its time interacting with the I/O devices.

The operation of the I/O devices is usually independent of that of the microprocessor, and a procedure must be adopted to synchronise program execution with their operation during data transmission. There are three basic types of input-output according to the method of controlling and synchronising data transfer:

(i)   Program-controlled I/O
(ii) Interrupt-controlled I/O
(iii) Direct-memory-access I/O.

The type of input-output used in a particular application will depend on three main factors:

(i)   The rate at which data must be transmitted.
(ii) The maximum time delay which can be accepted between the I/O device signalling its readiness to transmit or receive data and the data transfer actually taking place.

(iii) The feasibility of interleaving input-output and other microprocessor operations.

In this chapter, input-output operations using each of the three methods of controlling data transfer are described. The software techniques used to synchronise data transmission with program execution are explained, and the characteristics of each type of input-output are discussed. The hardware interconnection of the I/O devices and the microprocessor is described in the next chapter.

PROGRAM-CONTROLLED I/O

As shown in Figure 3-1, two basic types of information are transmitted between the microprocessor and the I/O device. These are *message data* and *control data*. The control data is used to synchronise the operation of the device with the execution of the program before transmission of the message data takes place. The input control data is called the *device status word*. The output control data is called the *device command word*. With program-controlled I/O, the input-output instructions are used to initiate and control the transfer of all types of data.

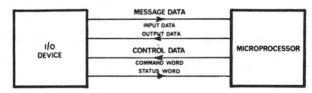

Figure 3-1. Information flow between I/O device and microprocessor

The status word is read into the microprocessor to determine the current state of the device. Each bit of the status word will indicate a particular device condition such as message data ready for transmission, device busy, device unavailable, or transmission error.

The command word is sent out from the microprocessor to control the operation of the device. Each bit of the command word has a particular function such as stop motor, increment feed, or change transmission rate.

The input-output instructions can be organised in one of the three ways:

(i) A unique instruction is provided for each kind of I/O data transfer using a single *device address* to define each I/O device. Typically, the four instructions are:

1) Read data (input message data)
2) Write data (output message data)
3) Send command (output command word)
4) Accept status (input status word)

(ii) Two I/O instructions, one for input and one for output, are provided for both message and control data transfer. Two device addresses are used to differentiate between transmission of message or control data for a particular I/O device. Typically, the two instructions are:

1) Read data (input either message data or status word)
2) Write data (output either message data or command word)

(iii) No separate I/O instructions are provided. The memory data transfer instructions are also used to communicate with the I/O devices by assigning a block of unused memory addresses as the device addresses. The approach is called *memory-mapped I/O* and is common in microprocessor systems which have a unified bus structure (see Chapter 4). Although the available memory address area is made smaller, this approach can reduce both program storage requirements and program execution times. The equivalent I/O instructions are typically:

1) Load data (input message data or status word)
2) Store data (output message data or command word)

In most microprocessors both message and control data are sent or received via the accumulator or some other working register. Some systems have special-purpose registers to deal with the control data or use the main processor status register for this purpose. Device status testing is simplified in the latter case since the conditional branch instructions can check directly the condition of the individual bits of the status register.

The control data is used to synchronise data transfer under program control in the following way:

(i)   A command word is written out to the I/O device to request transfer of message data.

(ii)   The status word is read in from the I/O device.

(iii)   The appropriate status bits are checked to test if message data transfer can take place.

(iv)   If the device is not ready, steps (ii) and (iii) are repeated until the I/O device is ready for data transfer.

(v)   The message data is read (or written) from (or to) the I/O device. This operation will reset the status of the I/O device.

Step (i) is omitted in applications where the decision to initiate data transfer originates from the I/O device itself. In this case, the device indicates its desire for data transfer by setting the appropriate status bits.

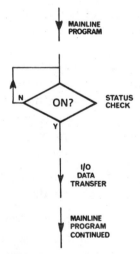

Figure 3-2a. Program controlled I/O (status loop)

In a simple program, the status check (steps (ii) and (iii)) is repeated continuously until the device is ready as shown in Figure 3-2a. The status check loop effectively halts the program execution and may cause an unacceptable waste of useful processing time. More sophisticated schemes, as shown in Figure 3-2b, where the status

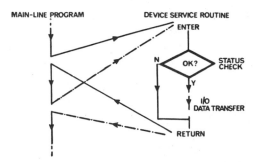

Figure 3-2b. Program controlled I/O (interleaved operation)

check operation is interleaved with other microprocessor operations, can use the processor time more efficiently. The problem is particularly significant in a microprocessor system which communicates with several I/O devices, since periodic status checks must be made on each of the devices. This *device polling* operation may also introduce a considerable time delay between a device indicating readiness for data transfer, and the program sensing that readiness and the data transfer actually taking place. In some microprocessors, the time spent in checking device status is

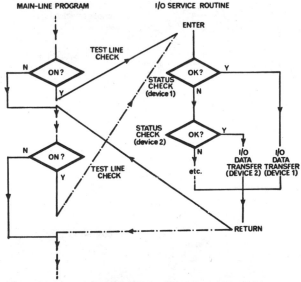

Figure 3-2c. Program controlled I/O (test line)

reduced by using a single test line. This line is common to all devices and may be used for signalling when any device requires attention. As shown in Figure 3-2c, the microprocessor can periodically and rapidly check the status of this one line and thus avoid polling the individual devices until one of the devices has signalled that attention is required. The time delay before servicing a device may still be considerable.

EXAMPLE OF PROGRAM-CONTROLLED I/O

A teletype is used as the output device for a microprocessor-based instrument. The results of data processing are first stored in a memory buffer and then written out to the teleprinter under

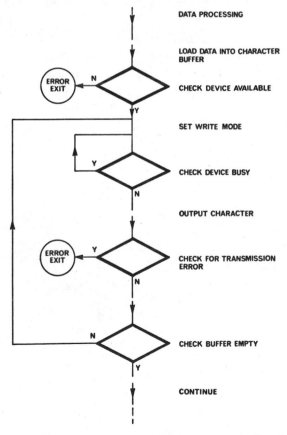

Figure 3-3. Program controlled output to teleprinter

program-control. A simplified flow-chart of the section of the program dealing with data output is given in Figure 3-3. The device status word and device command word for the teletype are given below:

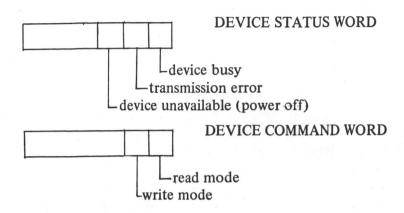

DEVICE STATUS WORD

device busy
transmission error
device unavailable (power off)

DEVICE COMMAND WORD

read mode
write mode

INTERRUPT-CONTROLLED I/O

The major disadvantage of program-controlled I/O arises from the necessity for periodically leaving the main data processing section of the program to check whether any device is ready for data transfer. The checking procedure, which must occur whether or not any device is ready, can waste valuable processing time. The problem is overcome in many microprocessors by introducing an *interrupt system* which allows the I/O devices to break into (or interrupt) the main program execution when, and only when, they are ready for data transfer.

In the simplest type of interrupt system, only one I/O device is connected to a *single interrupt request line*. The occurrence of a signal on this line causes the microprocessor to automatically initiate the following minimal sequence of operations:

(i)   Complete execution of the current program instruction.

(ii)   Store the current contents of the program counter.

(iii)   Load the program counter with a predefined program memory address.

(iv)   Inhibit interrupts and resume normal program execution according to the new contents of the program counter.

Thus recognition of an interrupt request signal causes a jump from the main-line program to a predetermined location in program memory (*the interrupt trap address*). In a simple system, with only one I/O device capable of generating interrupts, the *device service program* which controls the actual data transfer is loaded from the interrupt trap address. As shown in Figure 3-4, after completing the device service program, the previously stored contents of the program counter provide the *return address* to link back and continue execution of the main-line program. Interrupts are automatically inhibited before the start of execution of the device service program to prevent multiple interruption by the same interrupt request signal. In some microprocessors, the instruction causing the jump back to the main-line program also re-enables interrupts.

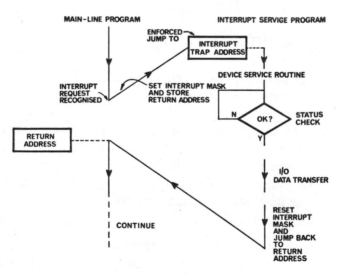

Figure 3-4. Interrupt controlled I/O

It is noted that the time delay before servicing a single I/O device under interrupt control can be longer than that occurring under program control, since the interrupt recognition, the hardware enforced jump and the store sequence require several machine cycles for completion.

Interrupts are inhibited by setting an *interrupt mask bit* within the microprocessor. In most systems the mask bit is part of the main processor status register and can also be set or reset by software. The mask bit is frequently used to prevent the interruption of certain sections of program which must be executed without a break (e.g., a section of data processing which must be completed before the next input-output operation can take place).

Many microprocessors use a slightly different interrupt system which employs a form of indirect addressing to link with the device service program. The interrupt trap address contains the address of the first instruction of the service program rather than

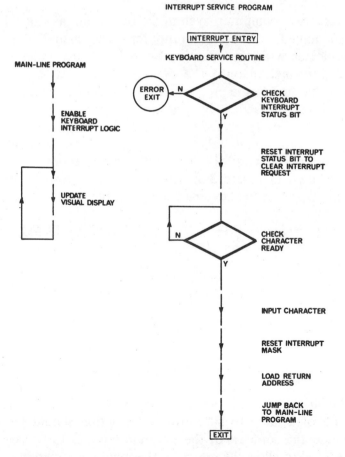

Figure 3-5. Interrupt controlled input from a keyboard

the instruction itself. The interrupt hardware automatically loads this address into the program counter before resuming normal program execution as described before. Indirect addressing allows the service program to be located at any arbitrary position in program memory. If the interrupt trap address refers to a location in read/write memory, the service program entry point can be changed during execution of the main-line program and the response of the microprocessor to an interrupt request varied accordingly.

EXAMPLE OF INTERRUPT-CONTROLLED I/O

An interactive computer system is based on a visual-display-terminal linked to a microcomputer. The main-line program communicates with the operator by writing out, under program control, information onto the display screen. At any time the operator can modify the program flow and change the information presented on the screen by entering control characters at the keyboard. An interrupt request is generated whenever a key is depressed. Data input takes place under interrupt-control. A simplified flow-chart of the interrupt driven section of the program is shown in Figure 3-5. The device status word and device command word for the keyboard are given below:

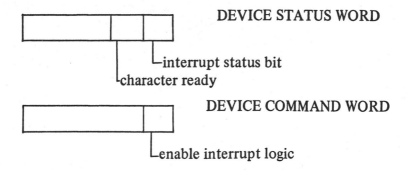

The similarity between the interrupt service sequence and the execution of a jump to subroutine instruction should be noted. Both cause the contents of the program counter to be saved and then restored to allow the return to the main-line program.

When the service program uses or modifies the internal working registers of the microprocessor (accumulators, index registers, status register, etc.), the main-line program execution could be upset since, unless the service program makes provision to save and restore the contents of these registers, they would be altered following the interrupt service. More sophisticated interrupt systems use the stack to automatically save the contents of the important internal registers as well as the program counter in response to an interrupt. Before the microprocessor resumes main-line program execution, the contents of the registers are automatically restored to their original values by the return jump instruction. The more registers automatically stored in this way, the longer will be the *interrupt response time*, i.e., the time between initial recognition of an interrupt request and the execution of the first instruction in the service program.

A more rapid interrupt response time is provided by microprocessors which have an architecture specially designed to facilitate interrupt operation. Some have two sets of internal registers. The main-line program is executed using one set whilst the service program uses the other set so as to prevent interference. Other microprocessors use locations in data memory to replace some of the usual internal registers. A single internal register, the work space pointer register, defines the memory locations to be used. The interrupt hardware stores and modifies the contents of the pointer register before executing the service program and thus defines a different workspace in data memory to that used by the main-line program. The pointer register is restored to its original value following completion of the service program.

REAL-TIME OPERATION

In many applications, the input-output is required to take place at a particular instant in time or periodically with a given time interval. In these cases, the operation of the I/O device and the execution of the program controlling data transfer must be synchronised in real-time.

The synchronisation is achieved by connecting an external pulse generator of known and constant frequency to the interrupt request line. The program is interrupted periodically with a known time between interrupts. The input-output operations can be synchronised to "real-time" by counting the interrupt requests and controlling program flow accordingly. Used in this way, the external pulse generator, which usually consists of a high frequency oscillator (typically about 1MHz) feeding a chain of frequency dividers, is called a *real-time clock*. Programmable real-time clock chips, which also allow software control of the clock interrupt rate, are provided in some microprocessor systems.

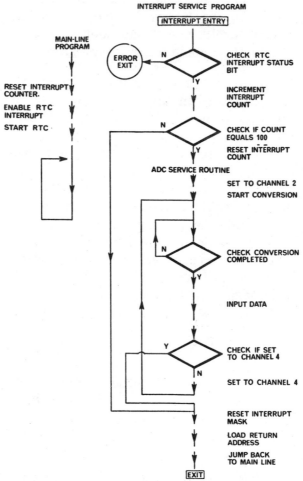

Figure 3-6. Program synchronisation using a real-time clock

EXAMPLE OF I/O USING A REAL-TIME CLOCK

An on-line data acquisition system is based on a microprocessor-controlled multichannel analog-to-digital converter. A 50Hz real-time clock is used to control the sampling rate of the system. In one application, the analog signals on channel 2 and channel 4 are sampled, digitized and stored in memory at two-second time intervals. The simplified flow-charts shown in Figure 3-6 illustrate the program flow during data collection. The device status words and device command words for the analog-to-digital converter (ADC) and real-time clock (RTC) are given below:

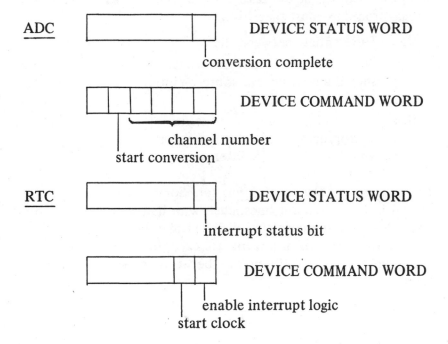

INTERRUPT SERVICING IN A MULTIPLE INTERRUPT SYSTEM

The simple interrupt servicing procedure described above is only appropriate in systems which have a single I/O device generating interrupts. Many microprocessor systems have more than one source and more than one type of interrupt. Three main types of interrupt may be defined as:

(i)   *External interrupts* generated from one or more I/O devices.

(ii)   *Internal interrupts* generated by the microprocessor system itself to indicate the occurrence of particular conditions or errors (e.g., power failure, system malfunction, transmission error).

(iii) *Simulated interrupts* generated by software to assist in program debugging or interrupt service testing.

The different sources of interrupt will have different servicing requirements. Some will require immediate attention; others will accept a delay whilst the task in hand is completed. The interrupt service procedure must therefore:

(i)   Differentiate between the various interrupt sources.

(ii)   Determine the order in which interrupts are serviced should more than one source of interrupt require attention at the same time.

(iii) Save and restore the contents of the registers of the microprocessor to assure program continuity during the servicing of multiple interrupts.

Recognising the source of interrupt. Some microprocessors have several interrupt request lines, each with its own unique interrupt trap address. The recognition problem may be solved by assigning only one source of interrupt to each line. This approach is commonly used to differentiate between internal, external and simulated interrupts.

In the majority of microprocessors several I/O devices must use the same interrupt request line. In these systems, two methods of recognising the source of interrupt are commonly used:

(i)   *Device polling.* The interrupt causes a jump to the interrupt service program via the interrupt trap address as described earlier. The initial section of the service program checks the status word of each I/O device in turn to determine which has caused the interrupt. Figure 3-7 illustrates the program flow of a typical service program for three I/O devices. The *interrupt status* bit, which indicates whether an I/O device has generated an interrupt request, is checked for each device in turn. The device status word is read into the status register of the microprocessor and a jump is made to the associated device service program if the bit is set. Device recognition by device polling is performed in software.

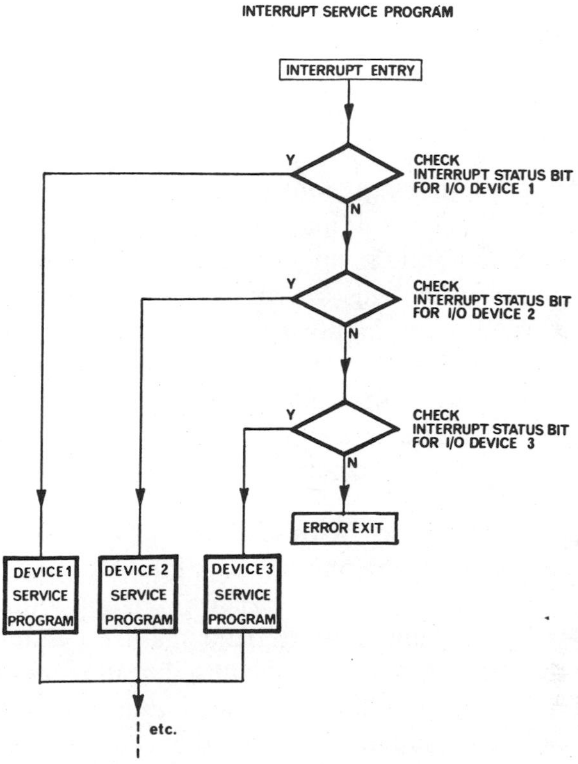

Figure 3-7. Device polling

(ii) *Vectored interrupts.* In the vectored interrupt micro-processor system, the interrupt control logic within the processor recognises the interrupting I/O device. Each I/O device is assigned a unique *device interrupt address* (not to be confused with the device address defined previously). On recognising an interrupt request, the interrupt control logic requires the interrupting I/O device to transmit its device interrupt address to the micro-processor. This address is then used to generate a unique interrupt trap address for the device. The trap addresses are usually located sequentially in program memory and form the *interrupt vector*.

Each location in the vector contains the start address of a device service program. The contents of the interrupt vector defined by the particular interrupt trap address are loaded into the program counter and program control is automatically transferred to the correct device service program. The process is simplified in some microprocessors by using the interrupt trap addresses as the device interrupt addresses.

In some systems, instead of transmitting an address, the I/O device is required to transmit a single byte instruction to the microprocessor after the interrupt request has been acknowledged. The interrupt control logic automatically loads the instruction code into the instruction register and normal microprocessor operation resumes by executing this instruction. Interrupt vectoring is achieved by using a special-purpose single byte jump instruction which derives the jump address from a part of the instruction code itself. Using the device interrupt address to specify this bit field, a unique jump address is defined for each I/O device. Device recognition by interrupt vectoring is performed in hardware.

Interrupt priority schemes. With several sources of interrupt there is always the possibility of one or more interrupt requests occurring during the servicing of an earlier interrupt request. In the simpler interrupt systems, the interrupt mask bit is automatically set when the first request is recognised. Subsequent interrupt requests join a queue. They wait until the service of the first interrupt has been completed before they can in turn be recognised and serviced. The order in which the queued interrupts are recognised is a critical factor in determining the time delay before service. The order or *priority* is dictated either by software or by hardware.

(i)   *Software priority*. After recognising an interrupt request, the service program polls the I/O devices in an order which determines the interrupt priority of each device. Thus the highest priority devices, which are polled first, are serviced first. Figure 3-8 illustrates the program flow during interrupt servicing with priority determined by software.

(ii)   *Hardware priority*. The interrupt control logic of the microprocessor sends out an external signal to control the interrupt

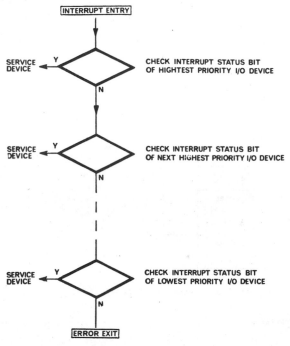

INTERRUPT SERVICE PROGRAM

Figure 3-8. Software interrupt priority scheme

request logic in each of the I/O devices. The control signal, which always reflects the state of the interrupt mask bit, passes through each device in turn as shown in Figure 3-9 (the daisy-chain structure is discussed in Chapter 4). If the mask is set, the signal will prevent all devices from generating interrupt requests. If the mask is reset and the signal arrives at a device which has no interrupt request pending, the signal is simply passed on to the next device. When the signal arrives at a device which is waiting for interrupt service, the interrupt logic in the device prevents the signal from passing on to the next device and generates an interrupt request itself. The position of a device along the control line will determine its interrupt priority. Thus, when more than one device awaits interrupt service, the device which receives the control signal first will be serviced first. Figure 3-10 illustrates the program flow during interrupt service.

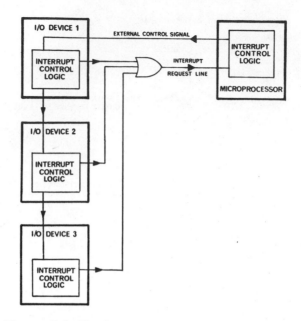

Figure 3-9. Hardware interrupt priority scheme

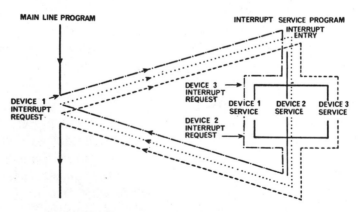

Figure 3-10. Program flow during hardware priority interrupt servicing

Both of these simple interrupt priority schemes are slow to respond to a high priority interrupt if it occurs during the servicing of a low priority interrupt.

More sophisticated schemes for software control of interrupt priority are used in microprocessors which have separate interrupt mask bits for each of several interrupt request lines or for each of the interrupting I/O devices. In the latter case, the mask bits are often included in the interrupt logic of the I/O device itself. By setting and resetting the individual mask bits under program control, a number of schemes are possible in which interrupt priorities are changed during program execution.

Many microprocessors have two interrupt request lines. One line has a conventional software controlled mask bit whilst the other is permanently enabled. This *non-maskable interrupt request line* has the highest interrupt priority and is used in applications which require immediate service at all times under all circumstances. An example of this would be the orderly shut-down of the micro-processor system following detection of a power failure. The simulated interrupt also has no mask bit, but since it is generated by a program instruction it has the lowest interrupt priority.

In some vectored interrupt systems, the interrupt priorities are automatically defined and controlled by the interrupt control logic of the microprocessor. After an interrupt request has occurred and the device interrupt address has been transmitted to the microprocessor, the address is compared with a multi-bit interrupt enabling mask. If the device interrupt address is equal to or less than the mask, the interrupt request is recognised, the mask is

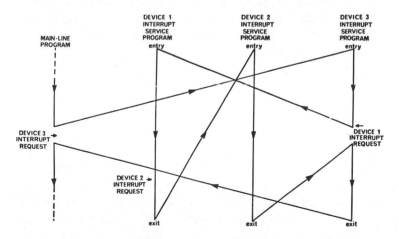

Figure 3-11. Program flow during vectored auto-matic priority interrupt servicing

forced to a value that is one less than the device interrupt address, and device servicing begins. If the device address is greater than the enabling mask, the interrupt request is queued. Only interrupts from a device with a lower device interrupt address to that of the device currently being serviced are recognised. Thus the device interrupt address determines the device interrupt priority; the lower the address, the higher the priority. The enabling mask can be initialised or modified under program control. Figure 3-11 illustrates the program flow during interrupt servicing. Here the interrupts are nested to ensure rapid service of high priority interrupts even if they occur during the servicing of a low priority interrupt.

MAINTAINING PROGRAM CONTINUITY DURING MULTIPLE INTERRUPT SERVICE

In general, the problem of maintaining program continuity in a multiple interrupt environment is similar to but more complex than that described previously for the single interrupt case. In particular, where nesting of interrupts occurs, provision must be made to save (and subsequently restore) the contents of all important microprocessor registers, including the return address held in the program counter, for each of the different interrupt requests which are currently being serviced. Each level of interrupt service requires its own unique storage locations in which the information can be saved. The save and restore operations are implemented in one of three basic ways:

(i)   *Program-controlled save and restore.* The information is transferred to a unique area of memory under program control in a non-interruptable section at the beginning of each interrupt service program before the interrupt mask is reset to allow recognition of further higher priority interrupts. The information is similarly restored in a non-interruptable section at the conclusion of each service program. In some microprocessors, the stack pointer is automatically advanced when an interrupt request is recognised and the programming can be simplified by using the stack as the storage area.

(ii)   *Automatic stacking.* The interrupt control logic automatically stores the information onto the memory stack and advances the stack pointer whenever an interrupt request is recognised. On completing the interrupt service, a special-purpose "return from interrupt" instruction restores the information and decrements the stack pointer appropriately.

(iii) *Special-purpose architecture.* The microprocessor is provided with several sets of processor registers and a pointer register to indicate which set is to be used during the current program execution. The pointer register is automatically incremented on recognising an interrupt request and decremented on completing the interrupt service. In some microprocessors, these sets of registers are internal to the microprocessor chip. In others, the microprocessor uses different workspaces in memory instead of different sets of internal registers.

The speed of response to an interrupt request, once it is recognised, is mainly determined by the time required to perform these save operations. Those microprocessors which avoid the need for information transfer provide the most rapid interrupt service response.

An example of a microcomputer using multiple-priority interrupt-controlled input-output is given in Chapter 9.

DIRECT-MEMORY-ACCESS I/O

Some I/O devices require data transfer at rates which are too rapid to permit any type of input-output which is under control of the microprocessor itself. In these cases, the information must be transferred directly between the I/O device and the memory of the microprocessor system without microprocessor intervention. The technique is called *direct-memory-access* or *DMA*. The data transfer is controlled by a dedicated high-speed logic circuit (the direct-memory-access controller) which is capable of operating at higher speeds than the microprocessor. During DMA data transfer, the microprocessor must relinquish control of its memory and allow the DMA controller to take over. There are several ways in which the DMA controller can gain control of the memory:

(i) *Processor halt.* An external control line initiates an orderly halt in the operation of the microprocessor following completion of the current instruction. Since the memory control signals of the microprocessor are disabled in the halt state, the DMA controller can take over and initiate data transfer. After the DMA input-output has been completed, the controller resets the halt control line, the microprocessor resumes normal operation and execution of the next instruction commences.

(ii)   *Cycle-steal.* External control lines initiate a pause in microprocessor operation by suspending instruction execution within the instruction cycle. The processor clock is halted and the memory control lines of the microprocessor are disabled. The DMA controller takes over and "steals" several machine cycles to allow data transfer to take place. On completing the data transfer the pause control lines are reset, the clock restarts, and the instruction cycle continues to complete the execution of the instruction. The only result of "interrupting" the instruction execution is to extend the apparent execution time.

Microprocessors which use dynamic memory (see Chapter 6) on the processor chip have a limit to the number of machine cycles which may be stolen in this way if no loss of internal status is to occur. Input or output of a long block of data may require several separate cycle-steal operations for completion.

(iii)   *Memory-sharing.* The memory is only accessed by the microprocessor at specific times during the basic machine cycle. At other times it is available for use by other devices. By synchronising the DMA controller operation with the processor clock, DMA data transfers can be interleaved with the normal microprocessor/memory data transfers within the basic machine cycle. Interleaved DMA has no effect on the operating speed of the microprocessor.

EXAMPLE OF DMA INPUT-OUTPUT

A microcomputer is linked to a large computer system via a high-speed communication channel. Blocks of data are transferred from the memory of the microcomputer to the communication channel by direct-memory-access. The main-line program, which communicates with the DMA controller using program-controlled I/O, specifies the data block and initiates the DMA operation. The DMA controller then halts the microprocessor and organises the data transmission from the memory to the channel. The simplified flow charts in Figure 3-12 explain the sequence of operations leading to the transfer of a block of data.

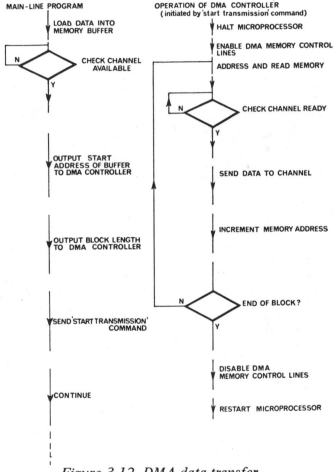

Figure 3-12. DMA data transfer

SUMMARY

The input-output scheme of a microcomputer is of great importance in the overall system design: a good scheme can give significant savings in both hardware and software. For this reason, a thorough understanding of I/O techniques is one of the corner-stones of successful microcomputer design. Most of the material covered in this chapter is applied in a more practical sense in Chapter 8.

Bus Structures and Hardware Interconnection with the Microprocessor

Chapter 4

INTRODUCTION

The microprocessor communicates with other parts of the micro-computer by sending information along groups of signal lines called buses. There are several different types of information to be transmitted between the various elements of the system:

(i)   Program memory addresses
(ii)   Instruction codes
(iii)   Data memory addresses
(iv)   Data from memory
(v)   Data to memory
(vi)   Input-output device addresses
(vii)   Data to output devices
(viii) Data from input devices.

In a large computer system each type of information might be transmitted along its own bus. In a microcomputer, it is common for more than one type of information to share the same bus. Figure 4-1 shows the bus structure of the simple microcomputer used as an example in Chapter 1. It has two *shared buses* along which different types of information are transmitted at different times. The instruction codes from program memory and the data from data memory share the same input bus; the program memory and data memory addresses share the same address bus.

The need for introducing a shared bus system is a direct consequence of the limited number of external pin connections that are feasible on a standard integrated circuit package. Although the maximum pin count has increased from 16 in the early seventies to 64 in the most recent microprocessor chips, some data multiplexing is always necessary to reduce the number of interconnections that are required. There are many possible ways of multiplexing the different types of information and a wide variety of bus structures are commonly used in microcomputers. In this chapter, the basic types of bus structures are explained, examples of the common bus systems are described and the methods used to interconnect memory and I/O devices to the microprocessor via the buses are discussed.

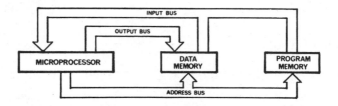

Figure 4-1. A simple shared bus microcomputer system

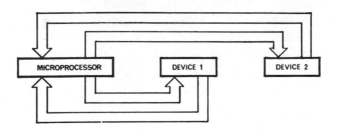

Figure 4-2a. Unique line bus structure

BASIC TYPES OF BUS STRUCTURES

The most fundamental bus structure is shown in Figure 4-2a. Each device in the system is linked to the microprocessor by unique signal lines. The structure is functionally simple, but expensive in external interconnections particularly on the microprocessor chip. There are two types of multiplexed bus structures based on the shared bus principle:

(i)   *The daisy-chain structure*. As shown in Figure 4-2b, the information is transmitted through each element of the system in turn along a loop of *unidirectional buses* until it arrives at the correct device. Each device must act as a source and an acceptor of information on the bus.

(ii)   *The party-line structure*. Each device of the system is linked directly to a single bus as shown in Figure 4-2c. When only one device acts as a source of information, the bus is unidirectional. More frequently the party-line structure is based on a *bidirectional bus* with information passing in either direction along the bus between a number of sources and acceptors of information.

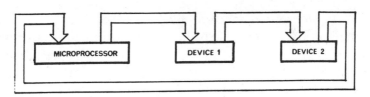

Figure 4-2b. Daisy-chain bus structure

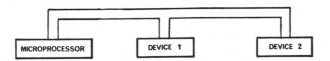

Figure 4-2c. Party-line bus structure

BUS CONTROL SIGNALS

In addition to controlling the rate of information flow on the bus, bus control signals are needed to indicate the direction of information flow on a bidirectional bus, to specify the type of information present on a shared bus and to define which element or elements of a microcomputer system are in control of the information flow on a party-line bus with more than one information source. There are two methods of controlling the rate of information flow on the bus:

(i)   *Synchronous control* (Figure 4-3a). One element of the system, usually the microprocessor, generates all the bus control and timing signals. The other elements in the system are required to synchronise to these signals when transmitting or receiving information on the bus.

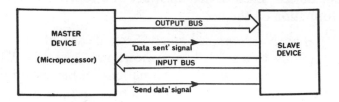

Figure 4-3a. Synchronous bus control

(ii) *Asynchronous control.* Bus control and timing signals are generated jointly by the source and the acceptor of the information transmitted on the bus. The *hand-shake* procedure shown in Figure 4-3b is often used. For example, the microprocessor might initiate the transmission of data from memory with a "send data" control signal, and then wait in a processor halt condition until it receives a response from memory. The response, a "data sent" control signal, is sent from the memory after it has placed its data on the bus. On receipt of the response, the microprocessor accepts the data from the bus and issues a "data accepted" control signal. The operation is finally completed by the memory which, after receiving this signal, removes its data from the bus and sends a "bus cleared" control signal.

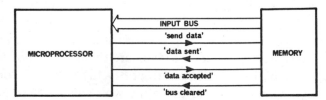

Figure 4-3b. Asynchronous bus control using a double hand-shake

The lines over which the various bus control signals are transmitted are frequently grouped together under one name — the *control bus.*

TYPICAL BUS SYSTEMS

The three basic bus structures described earlier form the basis of all microcomputer bus systems. All use the bidirectional party-line structure for the main data bus but the number and structure of the other buses differs from system to system.

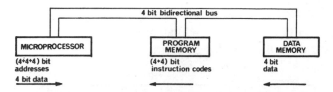

Figure 4-4a. Single 4-bit bus microcomputer

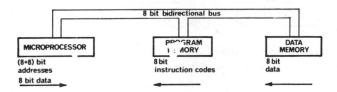

Figure 4-4b. Single 8-bit bus microcomputer

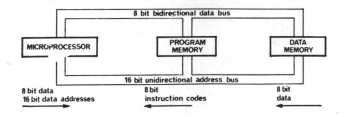

Figure 4-4c. Dual bus microcomputer

The single all-purpose bidirectional bus structure shown in Figure 4-4a was common in the first microprocessors where the number of external pin connections was severely limited (16 or 24 pins/chip). Frequently the bus was only 4 bits wide and instruction codes and memory addresses were split into 4-bit slices prior to transmission on the bus. The difficulties of demultiplexing the information on this type of bus are considerable. As larger numbers of pin connections have become feasible (40 or more pins/chip), microprocessors have been introduced first using a single 8-bit wide bus (Figure 4-4b), and then using two separate buses (Figure 4-4c). In the latter case one is an unidirectional bus for addresses and the other is a bidirectional bus for data and instruction codes. The dual bus structure with a 12- or 16-bit address bus and an 8-bit data bus is now an accepted standard for 8-bit micro-processors. However, a variety of bus structures is used in 16-bit microprocessors. Some have a single 16-bit wide shared data/address bus (Figure 4-4d), whilst others have separate 16-bit buses — one for data and one for addresses.

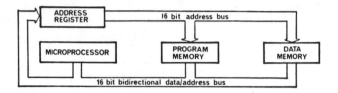

Figure 4-4d. Single 16-bit bus microcomputer with external address register

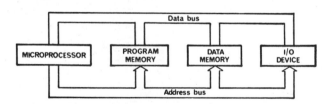

Figure 4-4e. Unified bus structure

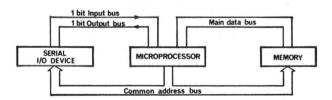

Figure 4-4f. Separate serial I/O bus structure

In most systems, communication with input-output devices is also made along the main bidirectional data bus as shown in Figure 4-4e (the unified bus approach), though several microprocessors have one or more separate I/O buses. Both serial and parallel I/O buses are now common as shown in Figure 4-4f and Figure 4-4g. Almost all microprocessor systems, whether they have separate I/O instructions or use memory-mapped I/O, use the same address bus for both memory and I/O device addresses.

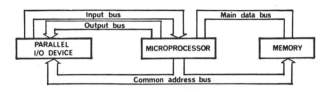

Figure 4-4g. Separate parallel I/O bus structure

INTERCONNECTING SEVERAL SOURCES OF INFORMATION TO THE SAME BUS

When information is supplied to a bus from more than one source, special bus driving circuits must be used to select and control the outputs from the sources so as to prevent interference between them.

The *bus drivers* perform three basic functions:

(i) They ensure electrical compatibility between each of the sources connected to the bus.

(ii) They control the connection and disconnection of sources from the bus.

(iii) They multiplex the information onto the bus.

Three different types of bus drivers are commonly used in microprocessor systems:

(i) *The logical-OR driver.* The driver includes a digital multiplexer which, as shown in Figure 4-5, is realised using conventional logic gates. Since one or another of the sources is always connected to the bus, this type of driver cannot be used with a bidirectional bus. The logical-OR driver is inconvenient in systems which have geographically distant sources and is difficult to modify if additional sources are to be added to the bus.

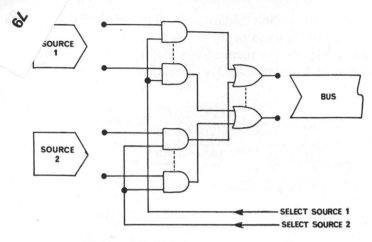

Figure 4-5. The logical-OR bus driver

(ii)   *The wired-OR driver.* In this driver the multiplexing is achieved by using open-collector logic gates at the output of each source. The gate outputs are wired together directly onto the bus as shown in Figure 4-6. The open-collector gates have the property that any one output transistor, if switched on, will override all other transistors which are switched off and so determine the condition of the common output line. Since the output transistors of sources not selected are turned off, the condition of the output transistors of the selected source will determine the data on the bus. The wired-OR driver can be used with a bidirectional bus since it is possible to select none of the sources.

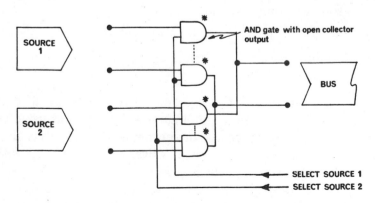

Figure 4-6. Wired-OR bus driver

(iii) *The three-state driver.* Special *three-state logic gates* which have active pull-up and pull-down output stages are used in the digital multiplexer. The output of the gates can be set in one of three states:

(a) Logical 1
(b) Logical 0
(c) High-impedance.

When the gate is enabled, the output is determined by the input to the gate. When the gate is disabled, the output is set in the high-impedance state in which the output line floats, acting as neither a source nor a sink of current. As shown in Figure 4-7, sources not selected are disabled and thus disconnected from the bus. The three-state driver can also be used on a bidirectional bus.

Since all sources of information must be connected to the bus via the same type of driver, the type of driver to be used on a particular bus will be determined by the microprocessor. The bus is often named according to the type of driver (e.g., open-collector bus, three-state bus).

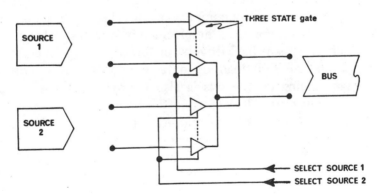

Figure 4-7. Three-state bus driver

INTERCONNECTING SEVERAL ACCEPTORS OF INFORMATION TO THE SAME BUS

When the information on the bus can be sent to either one of several acceptors, bus receiving circuits are needed to connect each acceptor to the bus. The *bus receivers* perform two basic functions:

(i)   They ensure electrical compatibility between the acceptor and the sources on the bus.

(ii)   They selectively gate the flow of information from the bus to the acceptor.

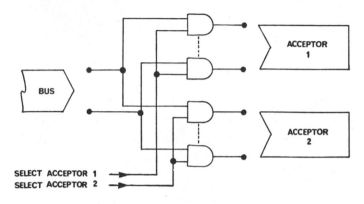

Figure 4-8. A simple bus receiver

Figure 4-8 illustrates the use of a simple receiver. The input gates, which are connected directly to the bus, are conventional logic gates of any logical family compatible with the bus. The maximum current loading on the bus is determined by the bus driver circuits. Most microprocessors have drivers capable of driving the equivalent of one standard TTL load on data or address buses. The total capacitive loading on the bus is also important since for a given source resistance, it will determine the bandwidth of the bus and limit the maximum speed of operation of the microcomputer. A maximum capacitive bus loading of approximately 100pF is typical for a microprocessor with a 2 μs cycle time. Bus receivers using special input gates can reduce the maximum bus loading, since the input lines to these circuits can be set in the high impedance state when the gate is disabled and the receiver is then electrically disconnected from the bus. The total bus loading is dependent on the maximum number of receivers which are enabled simultaneously. Some bus receivers use clocked latches in place of the input gates to incorporate a temporary information store (a buffer register) in the receiver. Figure 4-9 shows a 4-bit bus system with two sources and two acceptors using three-state drivers and latched receivers.

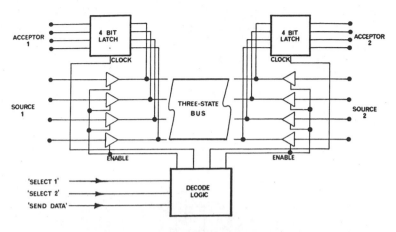

Figure 4-9. Bidirectional bus system

THE THREE-STATE BUS

Almost all microprocessor systems have one or more three-state buses. A number of special-purpose three-state devices are available to simplify the problem of interconnection with this type of bus. The *three-state bus transceiver* (a pair of interconnected bus receivers and drivers — see Figure 4-10) is often used as the basis of an interface circuit to link an I/O device to the bus. The *three-state latch* (a 4- or 8-bit data register with three-state output drivers — see Figure 4-11) is of general use in the design of bus interfaces. The *three-state bidirectional driver* (a quad of back-to-back bus drivers connected in parallel with complimentary driving directions — see Figure 4-12) is used as a bus buffer to boost the driving capability of a microprocessor which is connected to a heavily loaded bus system.

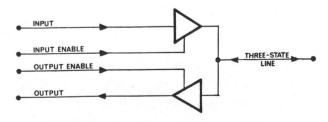

Figure 4-10. Three-state transceiver

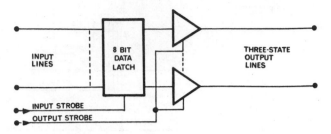

Figure 4-11. Three-state latch

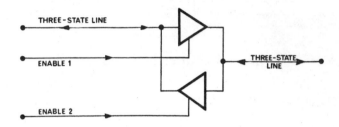

Figure 4-12. Three-state bidirectional driver

Specific examples of the use of these circuits are given later in Chapter 9.

THE MEMORY/BUS INTERFACE

The interface between the microprocessor and a memory array is required to perform three basic functions:

(i)   Ensure electrical compatibility between the bus and the memory array.

(ii)   Generate the memory-cell address.

(iii) Interact with the bus control signals to synchronise the data transfer to and from memory with the operation of the bus.

The complexity of the interface is determined by the type of memory array and structure of the bus system used in the microcomputer. Memory interfaces may be classified into three types:

(i)   *The memory interface chip.* At the time of writing, manufacturers of solid-state general-purpose memory chips have achieved some degree of standardisation in the organisation of the memory array (usually in 4-bit or 8-bit words) and, at least functionally, in the external connections. Chips with separate three-state data and address buses, and two control signals — chip select and mode control are common. Many microprocessor systems use a standard memory interface chip which is designed to link the general-purpose memory chips to their bus system. Figure 4-13 illustrates the use of a memory interface chip in a single bus microprocessor system with a single general-purpose read/write memory chip. Memory interface chips for dynamic memories also include automatic refresh control logic (see Chapter 6).

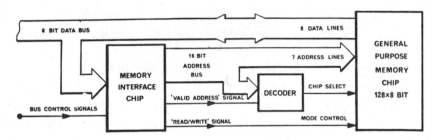

Figure 4-13. Memory interface chip

(ii)   *The special-purpose memory array with on-chip bus interface.* Because the maximum number of external pin connections per chip was very limited in the early single bus microprocessor systems, the rather complex bus multiplexing and demultiplexing logic required in the memory interface was often included with the memory array on the same integrated circuit. The same approach has been adopted in many of the small low-cost microcomputers where a minimisation of the total chip count is important. Figure 4-14 illustrates a typical special-purpose chip for a single bus microprocessor system. In some cases, even the logic circuits associated with memory access operations which are normally located on the microprocessor chip (e.g., program counter, stack pointer, memory address register, address auto increment/decrement) are also included on the memory chip. The distinction between the microprocessor chip and the memory chip becomes less clear in these systems. It is also common for special-

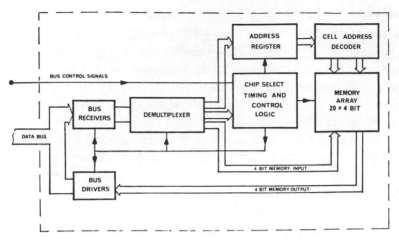

Figure 4-14. Special-purpose memory chip

purpose memory chips to have input/output lines, real-time clock circuits and interrupt control logic included on-chip.

The bus interfacing problem is very much simpler in a micro-processor system with separate data and address buses. Here the "special-purpose" memory chips only differ from the general-purpose memory chips in the chip select logic. As shown in Figure 4-15, additional interface logic is included on-chip to decode the most significant of the address bus lines so that a chip select signal may be generated.

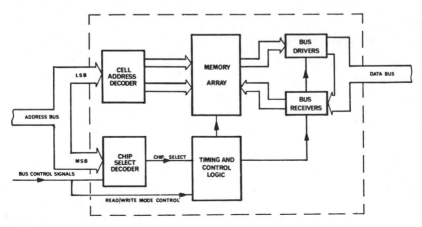

Figure 4-15. Modified general-purpose memory chip

(iii) *The special-purpose memory interface.* The memory interface will be relatively simple in a multiple bus microcomputer which has little or no multiplexing of information on the bus. In these systems the user can design his own memory interface, using standard random logic components to meet particular system requirements. Microcomputer systems which use large memory arrays or include direct-memory-access facilities are often more effectively designed using a special-purpose memory interface. The approach is unavoidable where the technology or structure of the memory array is fundamentally incompatible with that of the bus system. An example of the design and operation of a special-purpose memory interface is given in Chapter 6.

INPUT-OUPUT/BUS INTERFACES

Although the basic function of the I/O bus interface is similar to that of the memory interface, the design is often functionally more complex. There are two main reasons for the additional complexity. Firstly, the majority of I/O devices operate at relatively slow speeds in real-time and demand joint asynchronous control of the data flow through the interface. Secondly, many I/O devices are electro-mechanical in operation and cannot provide the degree of signal standardisation and bus compatibility found in semiconductor memory devices. In addition, some form of signal or code conversion is often required in the interface prior to transmission of data to or from the device.

There are many approaches to the design of I/O interfaces ranging from the use of special-purpose device-orientated input/output chips, where all the interface functions are performed on-chip in hardware, to designs based on simple general-purpose input/output circuits, where the special-purpose interface functions are realised in software. Five different types of I/O interfaces may be defined:

(i) *The parallel I/O port.* The I/O port is the most basic I/O interface and is little more than a simple I/O bus, either unidirectional or bidirectional, with latched three-state or open collector drivers on its outputs. Ports are usually 4 or 8 bits wide and are normally located on the microprocessor chip itself or on a special-purpose memory chip. Data transmission through the port is under synchronous control of the microprocessor and there are often no bus control signals associated with a unidirectional port. To avoid external multiplexing hardware, several ports are frequently used in the design of a single I/O interface. Figure 4-16 illustrates the use of four ports in the design of a paper-tape reader interface. The timing and control of the reader is determined by software.

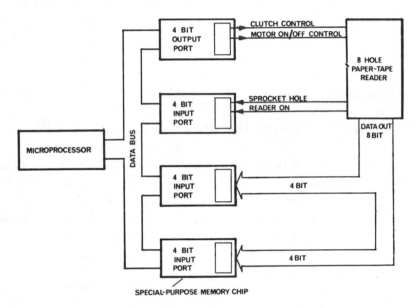

Figure 4-16. Simple paper-tape reader interface using multiple I/O ports

(ii)   *The serial I/O port.* The port consists of two single-bit serial data buses linked to the serial input and serial output lines of a shift register (8 or 16 bits long). The shift register, which is usually located on the microprocessor chip, can be loaded or read via parallel input and output lines, or shifted one bit at a time, under program control.

As shown in Figure 4-17, the serial I/O port is often used as a simple asynchronous serial data communications interface for a teleprinter. The shift register performs the parallel-to-serial and serial-to-parallel code conversion under software control. Alternatively, as shown in Figure 4-18, the operation of the port can be synchronised to that of the address bus to provide a number of parallel I/O ports.

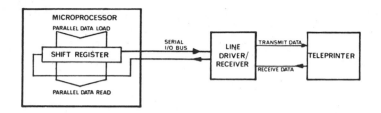

Figure 4-17. Serial I/O port used as a teleprinter interface

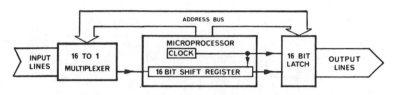

Figure 4-18. Parallel input and output using a serial I/O port

(iii)   *The general-purpose bus interface.* There are three basic types:

The *non-programmable* input interface, shown in Figure 4-19, performs the basic bus interface functions and includes some interrupt request control logic. It is similar in operation to the parallel I/O port described earlier.

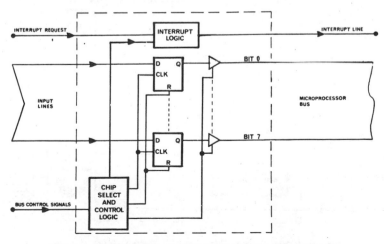

Figure 4-19. Non-programmable input interface

The *hardware programmable* interface, shown in Figure 4-20, typically includes decoding logic, several separately addressable parallel I/O ports and interrupt control circuits. External wiring determines the address, data direction and width of each port and controls the operation of the interrupt circuitry.

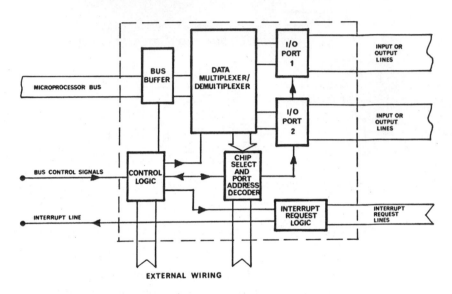

Figure 4-20. Hardware programmable I/O interface

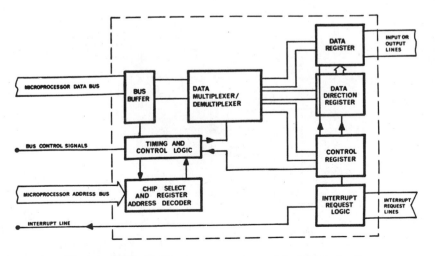

Figure 4-21. Software programmable I/O interface

The *software programmable* interface determines the structure and operation of the interface according to the contents of a control register which can be loaded by program. The interface shown in Figure 4-21 includes a second control register (the data direction register) which allows the function of individual I/O lines to be selected by software.

(iv) *The special-purpose bus interface.* The interface consists of one or more integrated circuits which are specially designed to link the microprocessor to a particular I/O device. In addition to the basic bus interface circuitry, the interface contains circuits to perform specific functions peculiar to the I/O device. For example, a keyboard interface would include matrix encoding and parity generation circuits; a lineprinter interface would include message formatting, character storage and print-head control and timing circuits; a communications interface would include serial-to-parallel/parallel-to-serial conversion, parity generation, message formatting and MODEM control circuits, etc. Unfortunately the lack of standardisation amongst the same type of I/O devices made by different manufacturers, and the high cost of developing special-purpose integrated circuits, has severely limited the number of I/O devices for which special-purpose interfaces are available.

(v) *The intelligent bus interface.* Intelligent (program-controlled) bus interface circuits were introduced to reduce the

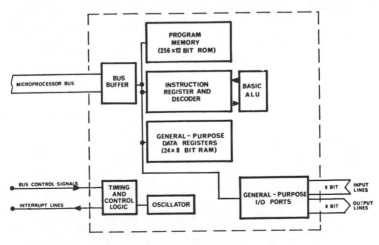

Figure 4-22. Intelligent interface

development costs associated with special-purpose interfaces. The intelligent interface, shown in Figure 4-22, is a simple single-chip microcomputer which has been specially designed with a limited instruction set to emphasise I/O control and interface operations instead of the usual general-purpose computing operations. The microcomputer has on one chip an external bus which is directly compatible with that of the host microprocessor system, extensive I/O facilities, and small data and program memories. The system is preprogrammed during manufacture to perform the interface functions required by a particular I/O device.

Off-the-shelf intelligent interfaces are available for a number of common peripherals (keyboards, magnetic tape cassette drives, printers etc.). General-purpose intelligent interfaces, which have user-programmable read-only memory on the microcomputer chip, can be used to meet the specific requirements of an I/O device made by a particular manufacturer.

SUMMARY

The bus structure of most microprocessors is determined by the integrated-circuit manufacturer and is fixed as far as the user is concerned. Nevertheless, it is important to understand the various types of bus structures that exist and their relative merits, because this plays a significant part in choosing a particular microprocessor and in designing the microcomputer system.

Internal Architecture of Microprocessors

Chapter 5

INTRODUCTION

Most single-chip microprocessors use MOS technology to obtain the very high packing density which is necessary to accommodate a complete processor on one integrated circuit. Unfortunately, MOS logic is relatively slow and faster operating speeds can be obtained with other types of logic systems such as Schottky TTL. However, these faster logic systems are not usually suitable for very high circuit densities and as a result it is necessary to build the microprocessor as a group of integrated circuits rather than as a single package. In breaking down the processor into smaller elements some other advantages accrue to the system designer. These include greater control over the instruction set and facilities for incorporating high speed logic techniques which are too complex for inclusion in a single chip device. This chapter attempts to explain the basic internal architecture of a microprocessor and to cover the various techniques which can be used when the MPU is split into several sections.

For the most part this text concentrates on what are known as "bit-slice" machines. That is, microprocessors which are available as a group of high speed circuit elements rather than as a complete MPU in one integrated circuit package. This makes it possible to adopt a more generalised approach to the subject as well as covering a class of microprocessors which, so far, have been precluded from consideration.

THE INTERNAL ELEMENTS OF A MICROPROCESSOR CIRCUIT

A microprocessor is built using three basic circuit blocks:

(i)   Registers
(ii) Arithmetic and logical unit (ALU)
(iii) Control unit

Registers can exist in two forms, either as an array of static memory elements such as flip-flops or as a portion of a random access memory (RAM) which may be of the dynamic or static type. Some microprocessors use both techniques on one chip so that, for example, the accumulator might be composed of static memory devices and all the other registers could be combined into a common dynamic random access memory. In addition to the registers which can be addressed and manipulated by the instruction set, buffer registers are often used for temporary storage of binary information which is being moved from point to point within the MPU. Clearly, a microprocessor which uses dynamic memory techniques must be continuously driven by clock pulses in order to preserve data integrity. Where all registers are implemented with static cells the train of clock pulses may be stopped without losing the stored information (see Chapter 6).

The arithmetic and logic unit usually provides, at the minimum, facilities for addition, subtraction, OR, AND and complementation. Shift operations can be accommodated either by the data selector approach, or by a shift register.

The function of the control unit is somewhat analogous to the puppeteer who manipulates strings so as to cause a puppet to dance the appropriate steps. With an MPU the registers and ALU form the puppet and the control unit is the puppeteer. For most MPU's the control unit accounts for more than half of the total circuit and is highly complex. The control unit uses a principle known as microprogramming to interpret each instruction and cause the processor to perform the required operation. Microprogramming recognises that, in order for the MPU to execute a single instruction, it must go through several steps. The full sequence of steps associated with a single instruction can be regarded as a small program — hence "microprogramming." The microprogram for each instruction is held in a ROM and as a particular instruction is received, the control unit calls up the appropriate microprogram.

A BIT-SLICE CENTRAL PROCESSING ELEMENT (CPE)

It is common in bit-slice machines to incorporate all the registers, ALU and other related circuits, into a single central processing element (CPE). But it is often impossible to include enough gates to form a full 8- or 16-bit word machine on a single chip, and consequently the central processing element is usually provided as a 2- or 4-bit "slice" of a full processor. Several CPE's are connected together to build up the desired word size in much the same way as 4-bit adders are cascaded to give 16-bit capability.

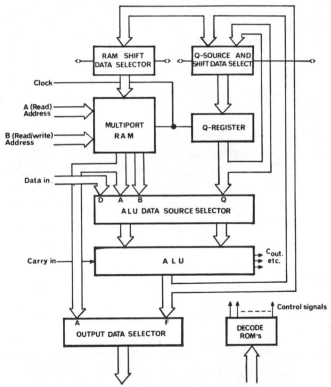

Figure 5-1. Typical 4-bit slice central processing element

Figure 5-1 shows a typical 4-bit slice central processing element. It consists of a multiport RAM which provides sixteen 4-bit registers, an extension register Q which is particularly useful for multiplication, division and other double word length operations, an ALU, two buffer registers A and B, and a read-only-memory (ROM) for decoding the nanoinstructions. A nanoinstruction is a single binary word presented to the CPE which causes the device to carry out one particular operation. The ROM decodes the nanoinstruction into binary control lines which are used internally to control the function of the ALU and the addresses of the multiplexers. It is necessary to use the ROM as a nanoinstruction decoder so as to reduce the nanoinstruction. Typically, the nano-instruction might be 8 bits wide, whereas the CPE may require control of 20 or more binary lines for each nanoinstruction.

The precise allocation and use of the 16 registers is defined by the system designer. For example, one of the registers would be used as a program counter, another as a stack pointer, and so on according to the chosen architecture of the machine.

A BASIC MICROPROGRAM CONTROL UNIT

Figure 5-2 shows the block diagram of a simple microprogram control unit. It comprises an instruction register which receives the instruction, a starting address ROM, a data selector which selects the address source for the microprogram ROM, the micro-program ROM, and a data selector which is used for conditional jump operations.

The instruction is loaded into the instruction register at the start of an instruction cycle and the op-code is mapped by the starting address ROM so as to specify the beginning of a series of micro-instructions which cause the full instruction to be executed. By using a starting address ROM it is possible to make more efficient use of the microprogram ROM and thereby reduce its size. Each word in the microprogram memory is known as a microinstruction and has three fundamental segments, namely, the nanoinstruction which controls the CPE, a next address for the location of the next microinstruction in the sequence and a condition code select address which drives the condition code multiplexer. An additional

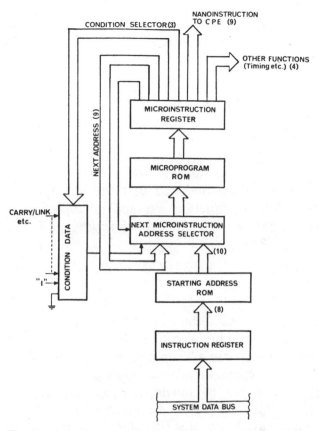

Figure 5-2. A simple microprogram control unit

single bit drives the microprogram address source data selector and usually a few more bits are required to interface with the timing and interrupt logic. For the first microinstruction in a full macroinstruction* the starting address ROM is selected as the ROM address source and thereafter each succeeding microinstruction uses the single bit control to cause the data selector to select the microprogram ROM for the next address. The last microinstruction in the sequence switches the data selector back to obtain the microprogram starting address of the next instruction.

---

*In order to distinguish a normal software instruction from a microinstruction, it is conventional to refer to the former as a macroinstruction.

The single bit output of the condition code selector supplies one bit of the next address so that the next microinstruction is selected from one of two possible instructions by the selected condition. For example, in Figure 5-2, when the selected condition is the carry-link bit, the next microinstruction can be one of two depending on whether the carry-link bit is true or false.

The size of the various addresses and ROM's in a microprogram control unit vary from one processor to another. However, in order to give a better appreciation of the approximate number of bits, some rough indication for an 8-bit machine is given in Figure 5-2. It will be observed that the microprogram ROM is quite large. Many instruction sets and microprogram designs are structured to reduce the size of the microprogram ROM.

ENHANCEMENTS TO THE MICROPROGRAM CONTROL UNIT

It is desirable to reduce the size of the microprogram ROM, not only for cost reasons but also to limit the overall number of pins and interconnections in a given design. Several methods exist for doing this. One common approach recognises that most instructions are carried out by moving through a sequence of microinstructions which are usually stored in adjacent addresses in the microprogram ROM. For this situation, it is adequate to generate the next microinstruction address simply by adding "1" to the current address and, under these circumstances, the amount of microprogram ROM storage needed to specify the next address is reduced. However, at the end of an instruction, it is usual to have an unconditional jump to the set of microinstructions which test for an interrupt before fetching the next instruction. In this, and in many other cases, it is necessary to specify the next micro-instruction address in more detail. This is done by setting the nanoinstruction to the CPE in the "no-op" state and using other bits, such as the condition select bits, to form part of the next address. The precise manner in which this next address is encoded into other address fields varies from one processor to another.

The power of microprogramming lies in the tremendous scope for specifying quite a long and complicated process, such as multiply or divide, in a single instruction. In order to realise this power it is advantageous to have the capability for one microprogram to use another microprogram on a subroutine basis. This can be done by providing the microprogram control unit with a stack for storing subroutine return addresses, in much the same way as a microprocessor uses a stack to handle normal software subroutines. For example, the microprogram for finding the square root of a number c, using the algorithm

$$x = \frac{1}{2} \left(x + \frac{c}{x} \right)$$

would call the division microprogram subroutine in order to evaluate c/x.

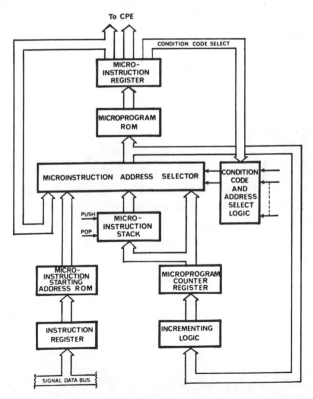

Figure 5-3. Typical bit-slice microprogram control unit

Some instructions, such as multiply and multiple-shift, require that the same sequence of microinstructions be executed several times. Usually a counter is used for this purpose, and at the beginning of the instruction the counter is loaded with the number of times the instruction is to be repeated. Each time the micro-instruction sequence is carried out the counter is decremented by 1 until, at the end of the sequence, the zero condition of the counter is used to cause a microprogram branch out of the loop.

Figure 5-3 shows a typical microprogram control unit for a bit-slice machine. Note that the address of the next microinstruction can be selected from one of 4 sources:

(i)   The microinstruction itself, as with the simple unit of Figure 5-3.

(ii)   An incrementer which adds 1 to the current micro-program address.

(iii)   The microinstruction starting address ROM.

(iv)   The Push-Pop stack used for storing microinstruction subroutine return addresses.

PIPELINING

Pipelining has been defined as "starting the next job before the current one is finished" but the precise application of pipelining to microprocessor design varies a great deal. Broadly speaking, pipelining consists of adding auxiliary timing registers at certain key locations so that memories can be addressed in advance of their outputs being required. This technique helps to reduce any system slow-down which occurs as a result of memory access time. For example, in the simple control unit of Figure 5-2 it would be advantageous to load the instruction register in advance of the beginning of the instruction cycle, so that when the cycle does begin, the microprogram starting address is already available at the data selector. In this way the access time of the starting address ROM does not add to the overall system timing.

A SIMPLE EXAMPLE OF A MICROPROGRAMMED PROCESSOR

Figure 5-4 shows the overall structure of a simple processor

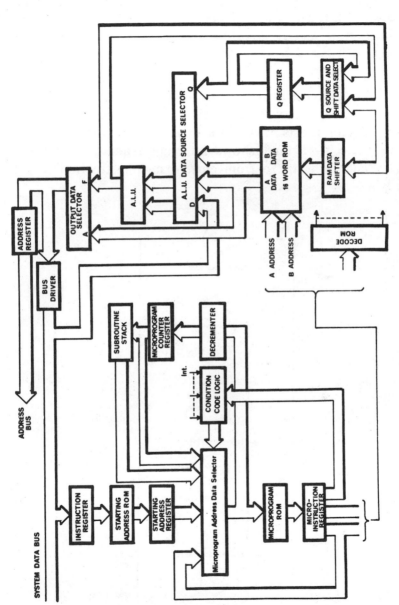

Figure 5-4. Simplified microprogrammed processor using bit-slice elements

operating under microprogram control. Each instruction follow the state graph of Figure 5-5. The loop of instructions, beginnin with State D through A and B, are the normal states followed b each instruction and it is convenient for explanatory purpose to begin with State D. The sequence of events beginning wit State D is as follows:

State D. Microinstruction switches condition selector t examine interrupt line. If line shows no interrupt, then nex address selector selects next consecutive microinstruction addres to give State A. If line shows interrupt request, next micrc program address is taken from current microinstruction to giv State E.

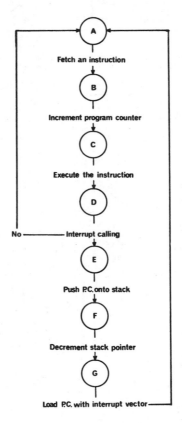

Figure 5-5. State transition diagram for simple processor

State A. Program counter contents are sent out on address bus and incoming data is loaded into instruction register. Microinstruction selects next consecutive address for next microinstruction.

State B. Program counter is incremented by 1 using the ALU and contents are returned via internal bus to the program counter. Microinstruction selects starting address ROM as the address for the next microinstruction.

State C. Execute the instruction.

After executing the instruction the microprogram control unit makes an unconditional jump to State D to begin the same sequence over again.

Specific locations in the 16-word processor RAM are allocated particular duties. A typical allocation might be:

Address 0   General purpose

Address 10   General purpose
Address 11   Index register 2
Address 12   Index register 1
Address 13   Interrupt vector
Address 14   Stack pointer
Address 15   Program counter

Then, for example, incrementing the program counter is done by placing address 15 on the B address lines, setting the ALU to perform the function B + 1 and taking the F outputs of the ALU straight through the RAM shift circuit and back into RAM location 15. On the positive going edge of the clock pulse, location 15 is loaded with the value (p.c. + 1). Incrementing and decrementing any register can be done in much the same way.

As an example of how a full instruction might be executed, consider the case of an interrupt. Normally an interrupt is initiated by an external event but some processors have a single instruction which causes the microprogram control unit to respond as if a hardware interrupt had occurred. The interrupt instruction, usually called software interrupt, is mapped by the microprogram starting address ROM to give exactly the same starting address as State D on the state transition diagram gives if a hardware interrupt exists. The first microinstruction places address 14 (stack pointer) on the A address lines of the processor RAM and the output data selector selects data bus A and passes this information to the address bus latch.

Hence on the positive going edge of the clock pulse the address register will be loaded with the stack location to be used. At the same time the program counter contents are incremented by 1 as detailed above. The bus structure allows the two jobs to be done concurrently. The next microinstruction in sequence is now called and this places address 15 (program counter) on the A address lines. The output data selector again selects data bus A and the main data bus transceiver routes this information onto the main data bus. On the next positive going edge of the clock pulse, this data (i.e., program counter contents) is written into the main system memory. The stack pointer is concurrently decremented by 1 by putting address 14 on the processor B address lines, setting the ALU to provide outputs (B-1) so that as the program counter contents are pushed onto the stack the stack pointer is decremented. The next sequential microinstruction also provides two simultaneous operations. Firstly, it takes the interrupt vector from location 13 and loads it onto the program counter (location 15). It places 13 on the processor address lines A and 15 on the processor address lines B. Secondly, it routes output A straight through the ALU and the shifter back into the processor RAM. Since the operation makes the next instruction address (i.e., interrupt vector) available on the A data bus, it is taken through the output data selector and loaded to the main address register so that the next memory address is set up well in advance of reading the next instruction. The microprogram control unit then jumps to State A to continue processing. In order to avoid an interrupt interrupting itself, one of the microinstructions in the interrupt handling microprogram usually sets a flag to mask off the interrupts.

Clearly, the microprogram for a particular processor is greatly influenced by the internal architecture of the processor itself. The simple example given above assumes quite a sophisticated internal bus structure so as to illustrate how one microinstruction can perform several tasks. However, many microprocessors have much simpler internal bus systems and their execution time is somewhat greater because data has to be moved from register to register in a more restricted manner.

The bit-slice approach gives the engineer much the same flexibility in computer hardware as TTL logic gave to the digital systems engineer. However, this flexibility is not always needed or desired and a more limited approach is often preferred.

MULTI-CHIP MICROPROCESSORS

In this section it is necessary to draw the distinction between bit-slice machines which allow variable hardware designs, and multi-chip processors which have a fixed hardware design but permit the user to specify the operation of the microprogram control unit by changing the microprogram ROM's. In its simplest form a multi-chip fixed architecture microprocessor consists of three circuits:

(i) The central processor which may have 8-, 12- or 16-bit capability

(ii) The microprogram sequence control logic

(iii) The microprogram ROM.

The microprogram ROM pattern can be changed quite easily so that the user has a great deal of influence over the way in which each instruction is executed. This ROM is often referred to as the Control ROM (or CROM).

Since the microprogram ROM has more or less complete control over how the processor executes each instruction, it is possible to cause the microprocessor to interpret particular instruction bit patterns in many different ways depending on the ROM pattern. This ability of a processor to behave quite differently according to its microprogram gives rise to the concept of emulation. This means that a processor is microprogrammed to respond as if it were some other processor. The emulator accepts instructions encoded according to the format of the processor which it is emulating, and interprets those instructions in exactly the same way as the original machine does. Thus it is possible for the emulator to run software developed for the machine which it is emulating. Many minicomputer manufacturers have used emulation to build low-cost microprocessor versions of their own machines, and thereby maintain software compatibility throughout their range of computers.

Another application for multiple chip microprocessors is in the design of special-purpose machines which require unusual instructions. For example, in nonlinear process control it is useful to have single instructions which evaluate polynomials or fit a curve to a set of points. These special instructions can be provided at microprogram level by encoding the program into the microprogram ROM and this method has the advantage that operations can be done much more quickly at microprogram level than under normal macroprogram software. A good example of this is the multiply and divide instructions available on some microprocessors; these instructions are an order of magnitude faster than the same program run in macroinstruction form.

SUMMARY

The internal architecture of microprocessors does not conform to some standard layout; it is influenced by many factors but it always contains an ALU, registers and a microprogram control unit. Careful attention to architecture can yield considerable improvement in instruction execution time and it is likely that advanced hardware techniques, such as pipelining, will be used more and more in microprocessors so as to obtain higher software throughput with the same basic semiconductor technologies.

Memories

Chapter 6

INTRODUCTION

A digital memory is an array of binary storage elements organised so as to provide some means of external access. The memory array is arranged as a set of *memory words*, each of which consists of a number of single bit storage elements or *memory cells*. Typically, a memory word has a length of one, four or eight memory cells and can store 1 bit, 4 bits or 8 bits (or a *byte*) of information respectively. The contents of a particular memory word are accessed by specifying a unique memory address. Since the memory address is normally decoded from a binary number, there are usually 2^n memory words in an array. The *memory capacity*, which is measured in bits, is given by the product of the number of memory words and the number of memory cells in each word. Memory capacities are frequently defined in kilobits (kbits) where 1 kbit = 2^{10} = 1024 bits.

There are two basic ways of organising the memory array to allow external access to the store:

(i) *Serial or sequential access* where the time to access a particular memory word is not constant but depends on its position (or address) in the array.

(ii) *Random access* where the time to access a particular word is independent of its position.

The *access time* is defined as the time delay between providing a memory address and gaining access to the stored information (the *read* access time) or completing modification of the stored information (the *write* access time). The speed of operation of a memory array is sometimes defined in terms of its *cycle time* which is the minimum allowable time interval between the initiation of successive memory access operations.

There are a number of different techniques for storing binary information. The memories commonly used in microprocessor systems are based on one of two storage techniques:

(i)   Magnetic storage
(ii)   Electronic storage.

Magnetic stores are non-volatile and retain the stored information when external power supplies are disconnected. There are two types: magnetic core memories and magnetic surface memories. Though the core memories have short access times (e.g., 400ns) they are uneconomic to manufacture for small memory capacity sizes. Typically, the smaller commercially available core memories have capacities of 32 kbits, and their application is usually limited to data and program store in relatively large microprocessor systems. Magnetic surface memories have longer access times (10ms to 50s) but provide a low-cost large-capacity non-volatile storage medium. Magnetic tape cassette and magnetic flexible disk memories are the most common secondary stores for data and programs in microprocessor systems.

Electronic or semiconductor stores are, with one exception, volatile and require the continuous connection of external power supplies if the stored information is to be retained. However, access times are short (30 ns to 500ns) and they have two major advantages over magnetic core memories:

(i)   They can be manufactured at a comparable cost/bit for small capacity units (memory capacities range from 1 bit to 16 kbits per integrated circuit chip) which can be assembled to meet the exact storage requirements of a particular microprocessor application.

(ii)   They are electrically compatible with the microprocessor chips and are more easily interfaced to the microprocessor system.

The use of semiconductor memories in microprocessor systems is widespread. In the remainder of the chapter attention is focussed on the various types of semiconductor memories. Memory cells based on the more important manufacturing technologies are explained, different addressing and accessing schemes are described and the various microprocessor applications are discussed. Two examples are presented to illustrate the design of complete memory systems based on semiconductor memory chips.

SEMICONDUCTOR MEMORIES

Semiconductor memories fall into three categories:

(i)   Read/write memory
(ii) Read-only memory
(iii) Read-mostly memory.

The contents of a read/write memory may be read out or modified an unlimited number of times under external control. The read and write access times are of similar length. In a read-only memory, the contents can be read out but, after they have been initially defined, they cannot be modified.

In a read-mostly memory, the contents may be read out but modified only with considerable difficulty. In this case the write access time is many orders of magnitude longer than the read access time. In addition, the number of times that the stored information can be modified is often limited.

THE BASIC READ/WRITE MEMORY CELL

Most read/write semiconductor memories are manufactured using either bipolar or metal-oxide-semiconductor (MOS) technology. Bipolar memory cells are *static* in that they retain the stored information as long as the power is applied to the circuit. MOS memory cells can be either static or *dynamic*. Even with the power applied, a dynamic memory cell can only store information for a limited period of time, typically 1 or 2ms, and requires its contents to be *refreshed* from time to time. Dynamic MOS memories have two important advantages over static memories.

(i)   The *standby power*, which is the power consumed by the circuit when read or write access operations are not taking place, is much lower.

(ii)   The number of transistors per memory cell is smaller. Thus larger capacity memory arrays can be manufactured on a single integrated circuit chip at lower cost.

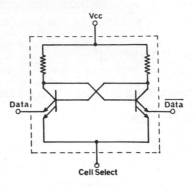

Figure 6-1a. Bipolar static memory cell

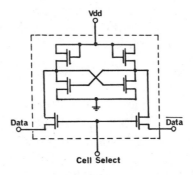

Figure 6-1b. MOS static memory cell

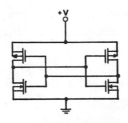

Figure 6-1c. Basic CMOS static memory cell

Figure 6-1. Static memory cells

A typical bipolar static memory cell is shown in Figure 6-1a. The two multiple-emitter transistors are cross-coupled to form a simple bistable latch. The connections to the emitters allow the cell to be selected and data to be entered or read out. Figure 6-1b shows a simple P- or N-channel MOS static memory cell constructed entirely from MOS transistors. Two of the transistors are cross-coupled to form the bistable latch as before, whilst the others are used for loads and for the gating logic which allows access to the cell. In both of these types of static memory cells, the standby power consumption will be high (typically 500mW for a 1-kbit array) since one of the two cross-coupled transistors is conducting at all times. The storage element of a static memory cell based on a complementary MOS (or CMOS) circuit is shown in Figure 6-1c. By using pairs of PMOS and NMOS transistors, a bistable latch is formed which has negligible power dissipation on standby (typically 1mW for 1-kbit array).

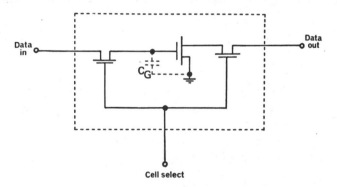

Figure 6-2. MOS dynamic memory cell

The MOS dynamic memory cell relies on the temporary storage of information as charge, or lack of it, on the gate capacitance of an MOS transistor. Figure 6-2 shows a typical design based on three MOS transistors per memory cell. Since the charge on the gate capacitance C_G will gradually leak away, the cell will require periodic refreshing of its contents. In addition, the data read-out operation destroys the contents of the memory and a data restore (read followed by write) operation is necessary to access each memory word. The periodic refresh operations, which are usually controlled by external logic, will reduce the availability of the memory for normal use. Typically, a dynamic memory is busy and unavailable for external data transfers for 1% to 5% of the time.

The restore operation which is performed automatically using on-chip logic will tend to lengthen the cycle time of the memory. Non-destructive read operations are possible in dynamic memory cells which are more complex and use more transistors than that shown in Figure 6-2. The read access time is thus reduced at the expense of a greater chip area per cell. In standby mode, power is consumed only during the refresh operations. The average standby power requirement is typically 2mW for a 1-kbit array.

ORGANISATION OF SERIAL-ACCESS READ/WRITE MEMORY ARRAYS

In a serial-access read/write memory, the sequence in which the information is loaded into the input of the memory will determine the order in which the stored information is available at the output of the memory. Access times are therefore dependent on memory location.

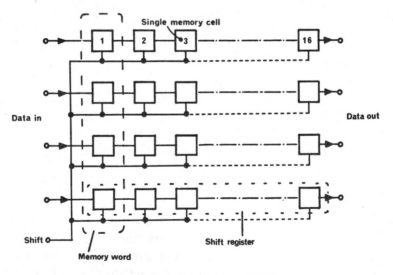

Figure 6-3. 16 x 4-bit FIFO

The First-In-First-Out (FIFO) memory. The memory consists of a number of shift registers equal to the number of cells in the memory word. As shown in Figure 6-3, each shift register which is formed by interconnecting a string of memory cells is clocked from the same source. At every clock pulse the contents of each column of cells is transferred one position to the right. New information is entered into the first column of cells and the oldest information is read out from the last column of cells. The entry of new information will lead to the loss of old information from the memory. Both static and dynamic memory cells can be used in the construction of the shift registers and the shift operation is usually controlled by a multiphase clock.

Figure 6-4 shows a memory cell from a MOS static shift register which uses a three-phase clocking sequence. The new data is read into the left hand side and the old data is read out of the right hand side of the cell when $\emptyset_1$ is high. The circuit operates dynamically during the shift operation and relies on gate capacitances for information storage. When $\emptyset_2$ and $\emptyset_3$ are high, the transistors are fully cross-coupled, the information is actively latched and the cell operates statically until the next clocking sequence begins. It is common for $\emptyset_2$ and $\emptyset_3$ to be generated on-chip from $\emptyset_1$. The maximum clock rate will depend on the charging and discharging time constants of the circuit. There is no minimum clock rate. A typical MOS static shift register has a capacity of 2 kbits/chip and a maximum operating frequency of 2MHz.

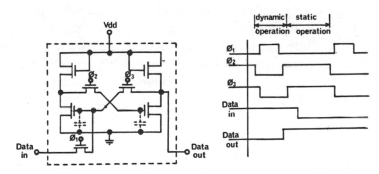

Figure 6-4. 3-phase MOS static shift register cell

Figure 6-5 shows a cell from a dynamic MOS shift register which uses a two-phase clocking sequence. The cell consists of two similar circuits interconnected as a master-slave combination. New data stored on C_{G1} is sampled when $\emptyset_1$ is high and its inverse is stored on C_{G2}. The data output line is set to the inverse of the data stored on C_{G2} during $\emptyset_2$ to complete the shift operation. The standby power dissipation is low since the load transistors are switched on only when $\emptyset_1$ or $\emptyset_2$ are high. Periodic clocking is required to renew the charges on C_{G1} and C_{G2}. The minimum clock rate (typically 10kHz) will be determined by the rate of charge leakage from the gate capacitors. The maximum time that information can be retained in the memory will depend upon the length of the shift registers and the minimum clock rate.

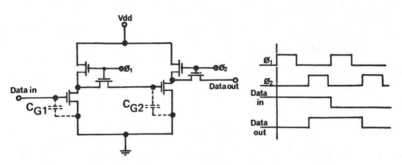

Figure 6-5. 2-phase MOS dynamic shift register cell

The recirculating memory. A recirculating memory is a FIFO memory with its output fed back into its input. As shown in Figure 6-6, some additional logic is required to allow new data to be gated into the memory. If the memory is constructed from dynamic shift registers, the recirculation operation provides a means of automatically refreshing the dynamic stores. In standby mode, the contents are continuously recirculated at a rate determined by the clock. In read or write mode the contents of the counter are compared with the address of the desired memory word until a match is found. The "write" or "read" control signal then gates the required data in or out of the memory. The access time varies according to memory location. It has a maximum value dependent on the length and clock rate of the memory.

As an example, a single chip serial memory fabricated with charge-coupled-device (CCD) technology, and consisting of 64 independent 256-bit recirculating shift registers, has a 16-kbit capacity and a $128\mu s$ maximum access time.

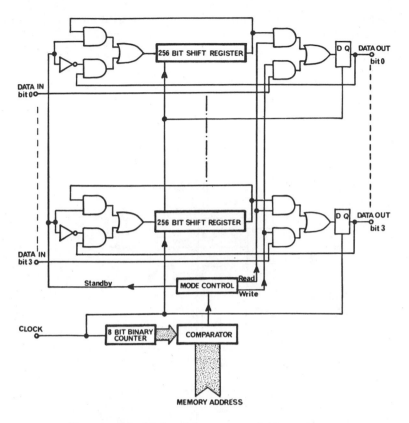

Figure 6-6. 256 x 4-bit recirculating memory

RANDOM-ACCESS READ/WRITE MEMORIES

In a random-access read/write memory, the availability of the stored information at the output of the memory is independent of the order in which the information was loaded into the memory. Access times are therefore independent of memory location.

The standard random-access read/write memory consists of a memory cell array with memory address decoders, data sense amplifiers, output buffers and access control logic, all on a single integrated-circuit chip. The term RAM is generally accepted to describe this type of memory although other types of random-access memory are in common use (e.g., random-access read-only memory). Memory arrays are based on bipolar or MOS static memory cells or on MOS dynamic memory cells. Two ways of organising memory address decoding are discussed below.

Word organisation. A multibit memory word structure is used in the array as shown in Figure 6-7. A single binary address decoder is used to select simultaneously each of the memory cells in the particular memory word which has been addressed. The number of external connections to the integrated-circuit package is high and the technique is only used in small capacity memories.

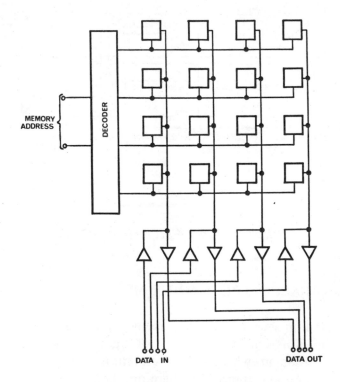

Figure 6-7. 4 x 4-bit word organised RAM

Co-incidence addressing. In larger memory chips the number of external connections is reduced by adopting a single bit memory word structure for the array. Two decoders are used to generate the X-select signal and the Y-select signal from the binary memory address. A particular memory cell is accessed when both of its X-

and Y-select lines are active at the same time. The logic to detect
co-incidence of the select signals is either included as part of the
memory cell (Figure 6-8) or is implemented using gating circuits
external to the array (Figure 6-9).

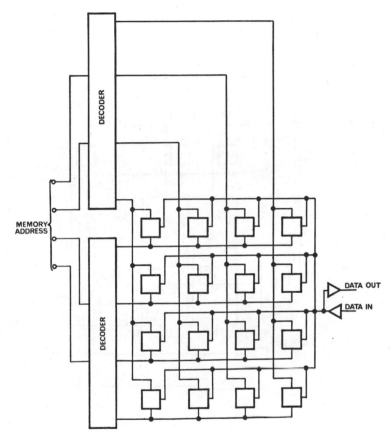

*Figure 6-8. 16 x 1-bit RAM with coincidence
addressing (cell detection)*

Most of the commercially available RAM chips include chip-select
logic and use three-state bidirectional data lines under control of a
read/write select signal to simplify the design of large multi-chip
memory systems. The number of words in a memory array may be
increased by connecting the outputs of several memory chips in
parallel as shown in Figure 6-10. The number of cells in each

memory word of an array may be increased by parallelling the address and chip select lines of several memory chips as shown in Figure 6-11.

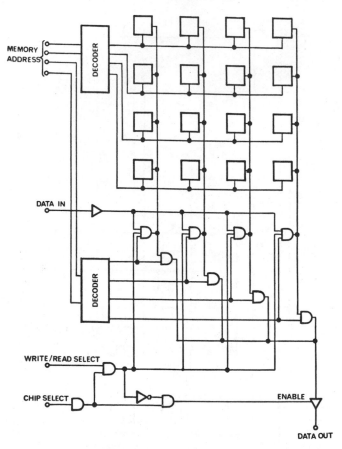

Figure 6-9. 16 x 1-bit RAM with coincidence addressing (external detection)

A typical bipolar static RAM chip has a capacity of 256 bits and an access time of 50ns. A typical MOS static RAM chip has a capacity of 2 kbits and an access time of 400ns.

MOS dynamic RAM chips have larger capacities (e.g., 4 kbits) and similar access times, but require additional external logic to control the refresh operation. In most cases, refreshing is accomp-

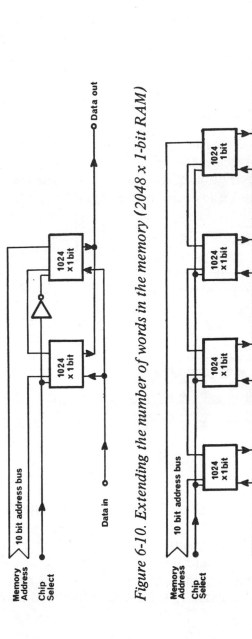

Figure 6-10. Extending the number of words in the memory (2048 x 1-bit RAM)

Figure 6-11. Extending the number of cells in the memory word (1024 x 4-bit RAM)

lished by performing a read or write operation, with the chip
select disabled, on each column of the memory array in turn. The
refresh operations must be organised so as to cause a minimum of
interference with the normal memory access operations. The
similarity between refresh and direct-memory-access may be
noted. A number of refresh control schemes are used. Figure 6-12
shows the important elements of the external control logic and
indicates the availability of the memory when using interleaved
cycle-steal and burst-refresh control schemes. All the schemes are
transparent to the microprocessor but only the interleaved refresh
scheme does not delay the normal memory access operations. A
more detailed description of a dynamic read/write memory system
with cycle-steal refresh control is given later.

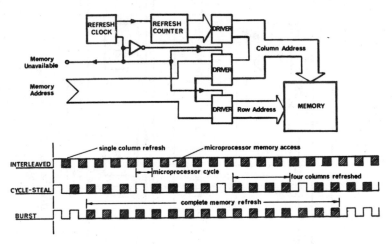

Figure 6-12. Refresh logic and timing

CONTENT-ADDRESSABLE READ/WRITE MEMORY

A content-addressable read/write memory (CAM) is a random-
access memory with additional logic included at each memory
cell to allow direct comparison of the contents of the cell with
externally supplied data. The CAM has three modes of operation:

(i)   Read
(ii) Write
(iii) Match

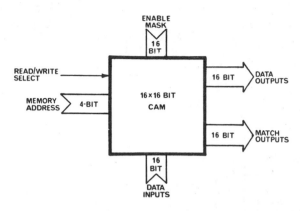

Figure 6-13. 16 x 16-bit content-addressable memory

In the "read" and "write" modes, the CAM functions in the same way as an ordinary random-access read/write memory. In the "match" mode, the additional cell logic is used to compare the information presented at the data input lines with the contents of the addressed memory word. Figure 6-13 shows the external connections to a simple 16 x 16-bit CAM. For each bit of the memory word, the results of the comparison are indicated at the match output lines. The bit enabling mask is used to determine which of the data input lines are to be compared with the contents of the memory word. Disabled data input lines are ignored. With additional external or on-chip logic, more sophisticated CAM's allow the bit comparison process to be made against the contents of every word in the memory in one operation.

The content-addressable memory provides a powerful tool for microprocessor applications involving data search operations.

READ-ONLY MEMORY

A read-only memory (ROM) is an array of memory cells whose contents are predetermined. The stored information is defined by the physical layout of the memory array circuits which then provide an involatile store. Each word of the memory can be accessed at random and its contents read out by selecting a unique binary address. ROM's use both word organised and coincidence

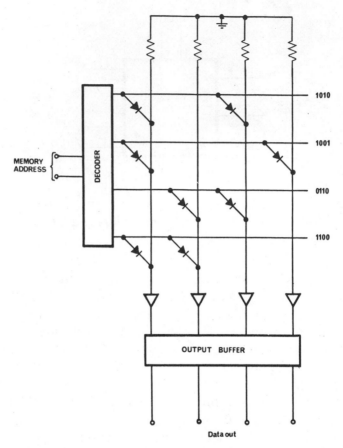

Figure 6-14. 4 x 4-bit diode matrix ROM

addressing schemes to decode the memory address. Although information cannot be written into the memory, the external characteristics of the ROM chip are functionally identical to those of the RAM chip. There are some ROM and RAM chips which are both electrically interchangeable and pin-compatible. The memory cell in a ROM array is simpler than that in a RAM array since its contents are unchangeable. Typically, the basic cell in a ROM array consists of a single diode or transistor. Figure 6-14 shows the layout of a small bipolar diode ROM using word addressing. The presence or absence of a diode at the nodes of the array determines the state of the memory cells. Similarly, the stored information in an MOS transistor ROM is determined by the presence or absence of an electrical connection between the gate and the row select line at each node of the array, as shown in Figure 6-15. In a bipolar transistor ROM the stored information is determined by the presence or absence of an electrical connection between the emitter and load resistor, as shown in Figure 6-16.

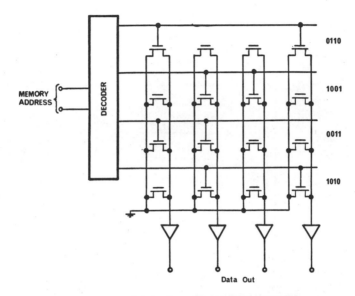

Figure 6-15. 4 x 4-bit MOS ROM

The bit pattern held in the ROM must be defined at the time of manufacture. Either a custom-designed integrated-circuit is manufactured or a standard integrated-circuit is manufactured and programmed at the last stage of fabrication with the desired bit pattern to produce a *mask-programmed* ROM. In the latter process, unconnected diodes or transistors are fabricated at every node position and then a special-purpose metalisation mask is used to interconnect the components according to the specified bit pattern. The mask-programmed ROM offers an economic method of manufacture when quantities are too small to consider custom-designed integrated-circuits.

Typically, single chip bipolar ROM's have 1 kbit capacity and 40ns access time, whilst MOS ROM's have 16 kbit capacity and 400ns access time.

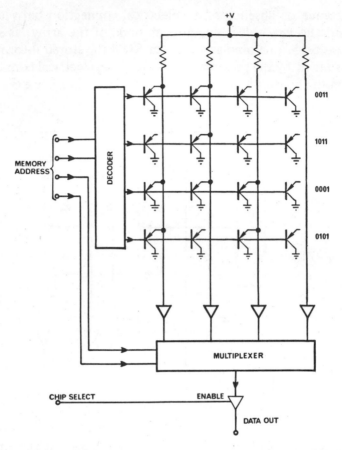

Figure 6-16. 16 x 1-bit bipolar transistor ROM

USER OR FIELD PROGRAMMABLE READ-ONLY MEMORY

The user programmable-read-only-memory (PROM) is a ROM chip whose contents can be specified after manufacture by external application of electrical signals. Two types of PROM's are in common use.

The fusible-link PROM. An integrated-circuit containing a bipolar or MOS ROM array is manufactured with all transistors fully interconnected so that the memory initially stores all 1's or all 0's in each of its cells. As shown in Figure 6-17, a critical interconnection is made at each node position by a fusible metallic or semiconductor link. The link can be destroyed to break the connection and change the state of the cell by application of an abnormally large current to the appropriate part of the memory circuit. The state of the cell cannot be modified once the associated link has been fused. The programming operation is performed in a special-purpose *PROM-programmer* which addresses a specified memory word and destroys the fusible links according to the bit pattern specified by the user. The programming of the entire contents of a 1-kbit PROM chip may take several minutes.

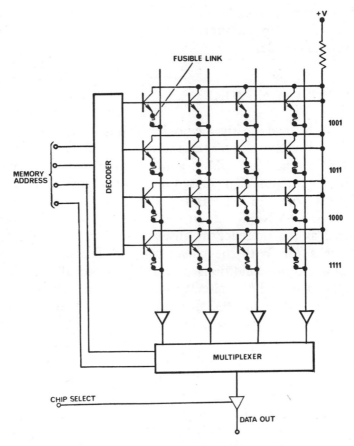

Figure 6-17. 16- x 1-bit fusible link ROM

The avalanche-induced PROM. The avalance-induced PROM is based on a bipolar ROM array and is manufactured with all transistors fully connected. By applying large external voltages, avalanche breakdown can be induced through the base-emitter diode junction of the transistor in any particular cell. A large reverse current flows, the junction fuses and shorts out the base-emitter connection to change the state of the cell. The programming is performed in a special-purpose PROM programmer as before.

There is some doubt about the long-term stability of user programmable ROM's. Some evidence suggests that it is possible for fused links or transistor junctions to reform by a diffusion process over a long period of time. Reports of such occurrences are not common and manufacturers of PROM's claim reliable operation over several decades.

READ-MOSTLY MEMORY

One type of read-mostly memory which is widely used in microprocessor systems is the user reprogrammable read-only-memory (RePROM). The RePROM is a read-only memory which can be electrically programmed, erased and reprogrammed several times. The most common type is the floating-gate-avalanche-injection MOS (FAMOS) RePROM. In each memory cell the information is stored as the presence or absence of charge on the gate of a MOS transistor. With the power supplies disconnected, or under normal operating conditions, the gate is electrically isolated from the other parts of the circuit and no charge leakage can occur. Unlike the dynamic MOS memory, the FAMOS RePROM can retain the stored information for a long period of time (at least 5 to 10 years). During programming abnormally large voltages are applied to the circuit. Avalanche breakdown of a diode junction allows charge to be injected into the isolated or floating gate of a selected memory cell. The programming operation, which is performed in a special-purpose PROM programmer, might take 2 or 3 minutes to load the contents of an entire RePROM chip. Charge can be released from the floating gate, and the contents of the memory erased, by exposing the circuit to an ultra-violet light source. The integrated-circuit is mounted in a sealed package provided with a quartz window so that the user can erase the memory in the field. The time to complete erasure which depends on the intensity of the UV light is typically 5 to 15 minutes. The number of times that the erasure and reprogramming operation can be performed successfully, though usually unspecified by the manufacturer, may be limited in practice.

FAMOS RePROM's are available which have capacities as high as 8 kbits/chip and read access times as low as 450ns.

THE PROGRAMMABLE-LOGIC ARRAY

The programmable-logic-array (PLA) is a general-purpose integrated-circuit which includes both read-only and read/write memory cells on the same chip. Initially the chip is fabricated with the various circuit elements unconnected. By specifying a final mask in the fabrication process, the PLA can be inter-connected to perform special-purpose memory functions. The incorporation of combinational and sequential logic elements on the same chip provides a flexible and powerful semiconductor memory element.

USES OF MEMORY IN A MICROPROCESSOR SYSTEM

Memories play a fundamental role in all microprocessor systems and have a number of different uses. Each type of application has particular requirements which will determine the most suitable kind of memory. Some more of the important applications are discussed below.

Main-program memory. The size of the main-program memory will vary greatly depending on the microprocessor's application. Typical capacities range from 512 bytes to 16 kbytes. The basic requirements are:

(i)   Non-volatile storage
(ii)   A read access time compatible with the normal operating speed of the microprocessor.

The most common types of main-program memory are mask-programmed ROM, PROM, RePROM or ferrite core memories. Dynamic MOS RAM with a standby battery power supply to guard against power failure is also used. Programs are often developed in volatile static RAM chips which are subsequently replaced by pin-compatible PROM chips. RePROM has obvious advantages during program development.

Microprogram or control memory. The control memory of a single chip microprocessor is situated on the microprocessor chip itself. The main requirements are:

(i)   Non-volatile storage
(ii)   High speed
(iii) Low power consumption
(iv)   Small chip area per cell.

The microcode will be stored in a ROM which is designed to meet these requirements and is fabricated using the technology of the microprocessor.

High speed and non-volatility are the important considerations when choosing a suitable external control memory for a bit-slice microprocessor. A mask-programmed bipolar ROM is commonly used.

Scratch-pad data memory. Scratch-pad memory is used as a temporary data or address store during the execution of an instruction or as a short-term intermediate store during the processing of data. In some microprocessors the scratch-pad is structured as a number of internal working registers. The main requirements here are:

(i)   High speed
(ii)   Low power
(iii) Small chip area per cell.

A dynamic MOS RAM is often used. A microprocessor using dynamic data storage has a minimum system clock frequency to ensure adequate refreshing of the data in the scratch-pad registers. The maximum number of machine cycles which may be stolen during DMA operations is also limited. There are no such restrictions in a microprocessor which uses a static RAM for the scratch-pad memory.

Some microprocessors use an external scratch-pad memory. The most important consideration here is speed and a bipolar static RAM is commonly used.

Main data memory. In most microprocessor applications, the size of the main data memory is small in comparison with the main program memory. In some applications, the internal scratch-pad memory will satisfy the entire data storage requirements. Large capacity high or medium speed data memories are sometimes required in microprocessor-based data acquisition systems where large quantities of data must be stored in relatively short time periods (e.g., a transient event recorder). In these applications MOS static RAM and ferrite core memories are frequently used. MOS dynamic RAM memory systems are also used; in particular, they find application in large capacity memory systems where the total power consumption and heat dissipation can be considerable.

In some systems, a small high-speed memory is used as a buffer store between the microprocessor and the slower large capacity main data store. Blocks of data can be transferred from the main data memory to the buffer or *cache* memory under external control so as to ensure that the high-speed memory always contains the data most relevant to the current microprocessor task. A bipolar static RAM is the obvious choice for cache memories.

Secondary data memory. A secondary memory or "backing store" is used as a long-term semi-permanent data store in a micro-processor system. The main requirements are:

(i)   Non-volatile storage
(ii)   Large capacity at low cost.

Access times from 5ms to 100ms are usually acceptable. The most common secondary data memories are magnetic tape cassette or magnetic flexible disk stores although the cost of semiconductor recirculating memory systems with battery driven standby supplies is becoming increasingly competitive.

I/O device memory. The microprocessor and its I/O devices usually communicate asynchronously. A temporary data store is often required to hold information during I/O operations. These I/O buffer memories, which are frequently included on the I/O inter-face chips, are usually of small capacity. In a memory-mapped microprocessor system, the I/O buffer memories are accessed in an identical manner to the main data memory. Most I/O buffer memories are based on the MOS static RAM.

Some output devices require a longer term data store of large capacity (8 or 16 kbytes) to hold the output data whilst it is presented to the outside world. MOS recirculating memories are common in devices which read out the stored data sequentially as, for example, in the character memory in a visual display unit (VDU). MOS static or dynamic RAM is used in I/O devices requiring random access to the stored data as, for example, in the character store of a line-printer.

Table 6-1 summarises the more important characteristics and lists the common applications of the different types of semiconductor memory used in microprocessor systems.

TABLE 6-1. SEMICONDUCTOR MEMORY CHARACTERISTICS

Type	Typical access time	Typical capacity chip	Standby Power	Volatile	Typical application
Recirulating	100µS	16k bits	medium	yes	character store
Bipolar Static RAM	50nS	256k bits	high	yes	scratch-pad
MOS Static RAM	300nS	2k bits	medium	yes	main data store
Dynamic RAM	300nS	4k bits	low	yes	main data store
Bipolar ROM	40nS	1k bits	high	no	control memory
MOS ROM	500nS	16k bits	mèdium	no	program memory

THE USE OF STATIC RAM IN A VOLATILE READ/WRITE MEMORY SYSTEM

A simplified block diagram of a 2-kbyte memory system is shown in Figure 6-18. The memory array consists of two banks of eight 1k x 1-bit static RAM chips. The ten low order bits of the address bus drive the memory address inputs of each RAM chip in parallel

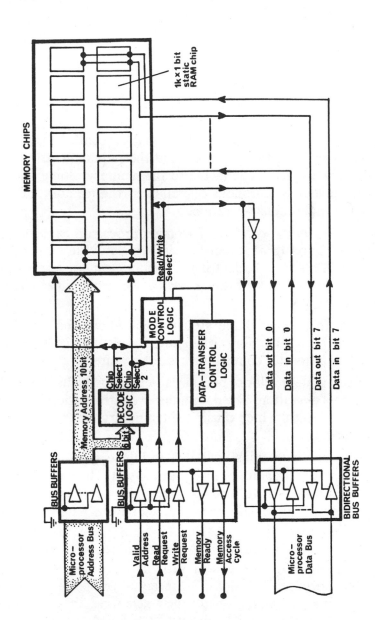

Figure 6-18. 2-kbyte volatile read/write memory system

through a set of bus buffers. The six high order bits of the address bus together with the "valid address" signal are decoded, according to the memory map of the microprocessor, to generate two chip select signals — one for each bank of eight memory chips. The bidirectional data bus is connected to the data-in and data-out lines of each RAM via bidirectional bus drivers. The mode select logic generates the read/write select signals for the RAM chips and controls the direction of data flow through the data bus drivers.

The design and operation of the data transfer control logic will depend upon the speed of the RAM and the requirements of the microprocessor which is connected to the memory. Some microprocessors demand synchronous operation of the memory; others provide for asynchronous operation.

Synchronous memory control. The microprocessor expects the memory to respond to a memory access request within a defined time interval. Data may be lost if the memory cannot respond in the required time. There are three ways of controlling data transfer when using a slow memory:

(i)   The frequency of the system clock is reduced until the microprocessor and memory operating speeds are compatible. Additional data transfer control logic is not required.

(ii)   The system clock period is lengthened during each memory access operation. The data transfer control logic generates a ' slow down'' signal which causes the temporary reduction in the system clock rate.

(iii)   Memory data transfer is treated in the same way as I/O data transfer under program or interrupt control. The data transfer control logic responds to and provides the necessary control signals to interact with the microprocessor during input-output operations.

Asynchronous memory control. After it has requested memory access, the microprocessor pauses with its operation suspended until a "memory ready" signal is received from the memory system. The data transfer control logic generates the "memory ready" signal from a delayed version of the "memory read/write request" signal. The delay is adjusted to suit the particular access time of the memory chips.

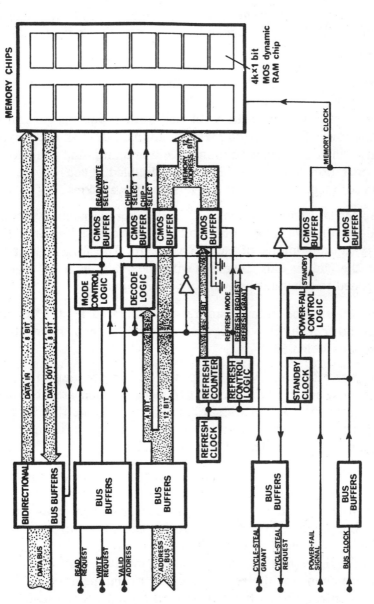

Figure 6-19. 8-kbyte non-volatile read/write memory system

THE USE OF DYNAMIC RAM IN A NON-VOLATILE READ/ WRITE MEMORY SYSTEM

A simplified block diagram of a 4-kbyte memory system is shown in Figure 6-19. The system may be considered in the four sections given below.

The memory array. The array consists of two banks of eight 4k x 1-bit dynamic RAM chips. Each chip is organised as a 32-column by 128-row matrix of cells with the column address generated from the lower 5 bits of the memory address. Refresh is achieved by addressing a particular column of cells and initiating a memory-write operation with the chip select disabled. Each of the 32 columns of memory cells requires refreshing every 2ms.

Chip select and address decoding. During normal memory access operations, the twelve low order bits of the address bus drive the memory address inputs of each RAM chip. The four high order bits of the address bus, together with the "valid address" signal, are decoded to generate the two chip select signals.

During refresh, the column address is generated by the refresh counter, both of the chip select lines are disabled, and the memory write mode is selected.

During power failure, CMOS low-power buffers are used to isolate the memory array from the control signals which are normally derived from the microprocessor bus. The address multiplexer and other parts of the circuit which must remain active during a power failure are also realised using CMOS technology.

Refresh control. Refresh is performed on a cycle-steal basis, one column at a time, under control of the refresh control logic. The refresh clock increments the refresh counter and initiates a new refresh operation every $62.5\mu s$. After gaining control of the memory by raising the refresh request signal, the control logic disables the chip select lines and initiates a memory-write operation using the contents of the refresh counter as the memory address. Memory control is then handed back to the microprocessor. The refresh logic, which must operate during power failure, is realised using CMOS circuitry.

Power-fail detection and control. The power-fail line is activated immediately a failure in the main power supplies of the micro-processor system is sensed. The power-fail logic allows completion of any current memory access or refresh operation before generating the "standby" signal which disables the chip and read/write select buffers and connects the standby clock to the memory array. The memory refresh control logic continues to operate normally as it derives its power from the standby supply. The total power consumption of the memory system during power failure is typically 200mW. If it obtains all voltage levels from a single 12-volt battery of 4.5 amp-hours capacity, the memory system could be supported in standby-mode for some 8 or 9 days.

SUMMARY

This chapter has presented an overview of memory systems rather than a detailed description of how they work. Hopefully it provides the microcomputer system designer with a guide to the various technologies at his disposal and some insight into their specific capabilities. For a more detailed description of memory technology the reader is referred to the bibliography at the end of this book.

A/D and D/A Conversion Methods

Chapter 7

INTRODUCTION

In order for the microcomputer to communicate with its environment, it is usually necessary to convert analog input signals to the microcomputer into digital format so that they can be manipulated by the microcomputer in its own "language". Similarly, digital output signals from the microcomputer often have to be converted into analog form so that they can be used and acted upon by external circuits. This chapter is concerned with the most common techniques used to achieve analog-to-digital (A/D) and digital-to-analog (D/A) conversion.

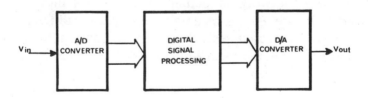

Figure 7-1. Basic method of using A/D and D/A converters

The relationship between analog and digital circuits is usually defined in terms of the number of bits used to specify a given range of signal values. For example, an 8-bit D/A converter can specify voltages in the range 0 to +10 volts with a resolution of 10×2^{-8} volts so that:

$$00000000 \ = \ 0 \text{ volts}$$
$$00000001 \ = \ 0.03906 \text{ volts}$$
$$00000010 \ = \ 0.07813 \text{ volts}$$

$$\vdots$$

$$11111110 \ = \ 9.9219 \text{ volts}$$
$$11111111 \ = \ 10(1\text{-}2^{-8}) \text{ volts} = 9.9961 \text{ volts}$$

A D/A converter is a circuit which, when presented with a binary number at its input, gives an output voltage proportional to that binary number. An A/D converter performs the reverse operation; an analog input gives rise to a digital output whose numerical value is a representation of the analog input. The analog/digital relationship is not usually one-to-one (e.g., 5 volts is not usually represented by 00000101), but some scaled relationship such as:

Full-scale analog input $= 2^n - 1$ when n is the number of bits available in the digital representation.

This chapter attempts to give a brief review of conversion methods and their applications to microcomputers.

DIGITAL-TO-ANALOG CONVERSION USING RESISTIVE NETWORKS

The resistive network is perhaps the classical digital-to-analog converter. Figure 7-2 shows an elementary form of D/A converter using binary weighted resistor values. It consists of a series of switches and an operational amplifier used as an adder. The switch for a particular bit is closed for logic "1" and is opened for logic "0." The diagram shows the position of the switches for the binary number 0011.

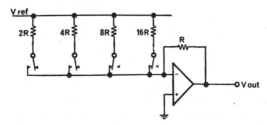

Figure 7-2. Binary weighted D/A converter

Unfortunately the system of Figure 7-2 is only suited to relatively low-resolution systems (5 bits) because it involves a wide range of resistor values, and it is difficult to match resistors in ratios greater than about 20 : 1. The R-2R ladder network shown in Figure 7-3 is more commonly used because the network can be constructed from only two values of resistor. Each switch is a single-pole double-throw type which connects the 2R leg to either the reference voltage V_{REF} or ground. This design has the disadvantage that the switches, which are usually semiconductor devices, need to be high voltage units capable of operating under difficult bias conditions. As a result the inverted R-2R ladder shown in Figure 7-4 is used in most contemporary designs because the switches run with a small constant voltage across them which makes for easier design and fabrication.

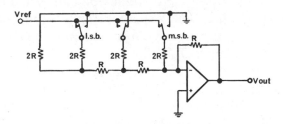

Figure 7-3. Standard R-2R D/A converter

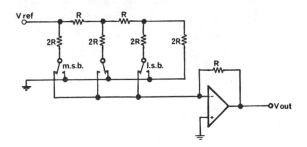

Figure 7-4. Inverted R-2R D/A converter

It is important to note that the D/A converter gives out a voltage which is proportional to the product of the digital input and the reference voltage V_{REF}.

If the reference input is connected to some analog voltage of interest, the D/A converter behaves as a variable attenuator (or multiplier) which is set digitally. In general, D/A converters which use bipolar IC components can only function with positive values of V_{REF} and then may only be used to attenuate a limited range of positive signals. Properly designed D/A converters using MOS analog switches can be used with both positive and negative values of V_{REF} and therefore are more suited for true multiplying applications where it is desired to multiply an analog signal at the V_{REF} input by some digital number.

DIGITAL-TO-ANALOG CONVERSION USING PULSE-WIDTH MODULATION

It is possible to perform digital-to-analog conversion by creating a series of pulses whose mark-space ratio is proportional to the digital values (see Figure 7-5). For example, in a simple 6-bit pulse-width modulated D/A, the binary number 011010 (=26) would be represented at the output as a continuous rectangular waveform with a "mark" width of 26 units and a "space" width of 63-26 = 37 units. The rectangular waveform is passed through a low-pass filter to obtain the dc signal output. A simple pulse-width modulator would be a continuously running binary counter feeding a comparator, the other side of which is connected to the binary value to be converted (see Figure 7-6). The comparator gives an output when the counter value is less than the binary value. The system has only limited resolution and a very slow response time due to the low-pass filter. It can be improved somewhat by replacing the counter with a pseudo-random binary sequence generator that generates exactly the same range of

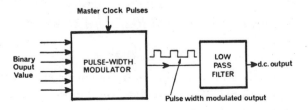

Figure 7-5. Pulse-width modulation D/A converter

numbers but in a random fashion. In this way the low-pass filter cut-off frequency can be raised and better resolution up to about 8 bits can be obtained.

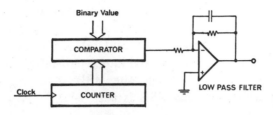

Figure 7-6. Possible hardware circuit for pulse-width modulated D/A converter

TRACKING A/D CONVERTERS

Figure 7-7 shows a tracking A/D converter. It consists of an up/down counter which drives a resistive ladder type D/A converter. The output from the D/A feeds one side of a comparator and the analog input V_{IN} feeds the other side. If the D/A output is less than V_{IN} the comparator causes the counter to count up on the next clock pulse and if the D/A output is greater than V_{IN}, the counter counts down. In this scheme the maximum track rate of the A/D is governed by the settling time of the comparator and the clock frequency. Tracking A/D converters can normally be used up to low-audio frequencies although it is possible to speed-up the conversion process by using "panic-mode" tracking where the counter is incremented in steps of, say, 4 units until the converter is in the correct range.

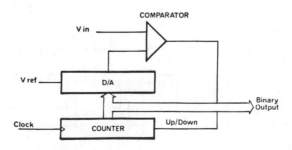

Figure 7-7. Tracking A/D converter

SUCCESSIVE-APPROXIMATIONS A/D CONVERTER

The successive-approximations A/D converter (see Figure 7-8) uses much the same logic configuration as the tracking A/D converter but the counter is replaced by a successive-approximations register (SAR). Successive-approximations is essentially a "try it and see" method. Initially the most significant bit of the SAR is set to "1" causing the D/A converter to give-out a half-range analog value. If the comparator output is high, the MSB of the result is set to a "1", and if it is low, the MSB is set to "0." The resulting MSB

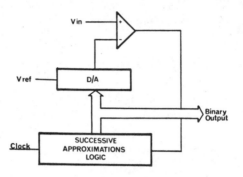

Figure 7-8. Successive-approximations A/D converter

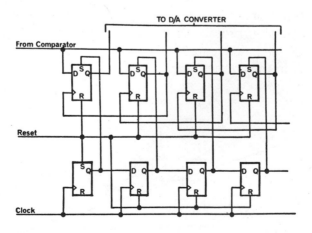

Figure 7-9. Successive-approximations logic

determines the D/A converter input and the logic proceeds to test the next lower bit in the same way (see Figure 7-9). This series of approximations continues until all bits have been determined. Successive-approximations is a very fast method of A/D conversion because for an n-bit conversion the conversion time is only n times the D/A and comparator settling time. A monolithic 10-bit converter like the AD571 can achieve a 10-bit conversion in less than $20\mu s$.

DUAL-SLOPE INTEGRATING TYPE A/D CONVERTERS

An integrating dual-slope D/A converter performs the conversion process by feeding the unknown signal to an analog integrator for a fixed period of time. The unknown signal is then removed from the integrator input and a reference voltage of opposite polarity is applied. The time taken for the integrator to ramp back to its starting point is a measure of the magnitude of the unknown analog input. Figure 7-10 shows the basic circuit for a dual-slope converter.

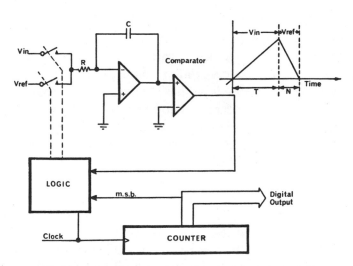

Figure 7-10. Simplified block diagram of dual-slope A/D converter

In practice, the counter is usually set to zero at the start of the conversion. When the counter has reached the all "ones" state and

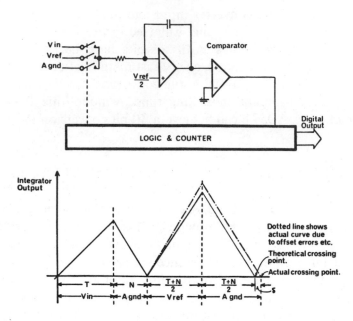

Figure 7-11. Simplified quad-slope converter

is about to proceed to the all "zero" state, the switches change over. Thus the counter is set to zero at the beginning of the ramp-down period and its accumulated count N is a direct measure of the analog input. Dual-slope has the advantage that errors are minimised because the same analog loop is used for both the V_{IN} and V_{REF} signals. In this way long term variations in the values of R and C do not affect the overall accuracy (see Figure 7-10). Unfortunately the circuit is sensitive to zero offset and drift in the integrator and comparator. It is normal to supplement the basic dual-slope with some additional circuits or logic to achieve compensation for these effects. One method is the Quad-Slope* approach shown in Figure 7-11. The circuit initially makes a dual-slope conversion on the unknown analog input and then repeats the conversion *over exactly the same period of time* using reference inputs. If there is no error in the analog circuits then the final ramp should hit the comparator crossing point after time (T+N),

*Analog Devices – U.S. Patent No. 3872466.

but if there is error then the crossing point will occur at some other time. Since this error δ has been accumulated over period (T+N), it is a measure of the error incurred in the first conversion process, and therefore the true value of N can be obtained by subtracting δ from N. The actual implementation of the quad-slope process is rather more complicated than would appear from the above description. There is increasing emphasis on methods which, like the quad-slope method, supplement the basic dual-slope process with addition calibration phases to measure the error and then use a microcomputer to remove this error from the original measured value. The error corrected dual-slope conversion technique enables high resolution to be obtained (the Analog Devices AD7550 achieves 13 bits), but because of the integration process, it suffers from the disadvantage of low conversion speed.

OTHER TYPES OF INTEGRATING A/D CONVERTERS

The concept of charging a capacitor from an unknown signal and then discharging the capacitor with a reference source can be applied in many ways. Some of the available techniques are considered here.

Charge-balancing A/D converters. With charge-balancing A/D converters (see Figure 7-12), the integrator input is switched repetitively between the unknown analog input and a reference source. This enables the integrator's output to be held within certain limits defined by the comparator hysteresis. The analog input value is found from the proportion of time within a given

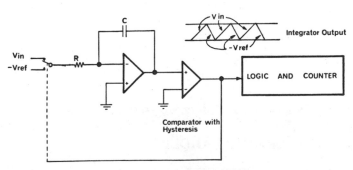

Figure 7-12. Basic charge-balancing converter

time frame that the reference signal has to be connected to the integrator input. In practice it is necessary to include a zeroing period prior to the measuring period. The charge-balancing method has the advantage that, as analog signal swings are small, the integrator operates over a small dynamic range. However, since the switches open and close frequently during a measuring period, errors that occur at switching points are magnified.

Voltage-to-frequency conversion. The previous charge-balancing circuit is a form of voltage-to-frequency converter since, as the input voltage increases, the ramp frequency increases. Voltage-to-frequency converters take several forms, but in principle most of them are of the charge-balance type. They operate by charging a capacitor from a current source which is proportional to the input voltage, and then discharging the capacitor with a precise current each time the charge on the capacitor reaches a pre-set level. This technique is shown in figure 7-13. Voltage-to-frequency converters have relatively poor performance for low input voltages due to offset voltage errors. In addition, there is an upper frequency limit imposed by the slew rate and settling time of the amplifier, but with careful design it is possible to achieve a dynamic range of better than 10^4. In order to accomplish A/D conversion, it is normal to feed the comparator output pulses into a counter for a fixed period of time. The accumulated count is proportional to the input voltage.

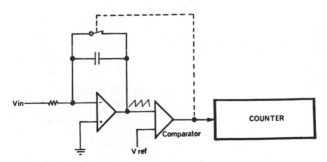

Figure 7-13. Voltage-to-frequency converter

MULTI-COMPARATOR LADDER

For high-speed low-resolution applications, it is possible perform the A/D conversion function by using one comparator for each possible level and feeding the input signal to all comparators. This method is shown schematically in Figure 7-14. Unfortunately it requires $(2^n - 1)$ comparators for an n-bit binary word. The comparator outputs have to be encoded into the appropriate binary word.

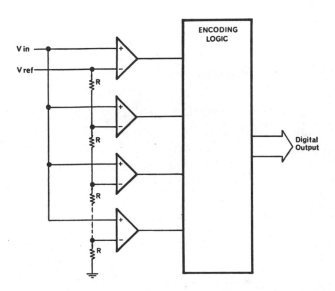

Figure 7-14. High-speed A/D converter using multiple comparators

D/A CONVERTERS USING MICROCOMPUTERS

In very low cost applications it is sometimes desirable to use the microcomputer for the D/A conversion function in order to avoid the expense of the D/A circuit. The pulse-width modulation type of D/A converter is particularly suitable for implementing on a microcomputer because it only requires 1 bit of output plus a low pass filter as shown in Figure 7-15. The microcomputer achieves the counter and comparator function of Figure 7-6 by means of software and it increments the counter at regular intervals. Usually the increment points are determined by a real-time clock which drives the microcomputer interrupt system. As long as the "counter" contents are less than the desired output value, the output bit is set to a "1" and once the counter is greater than the desired value, the output bit is set to a "0".

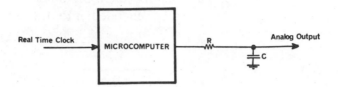

Figure 7-15. Pulse-width modulation D/A conversion using a single bit output from a microcomputer

This method of D/A conversion involves a significant amount of software time and can only be used where the microcomputer is not heavily taxed with other tasks. In addition, it has poor resolution and the apparent saving in external circuits is usually lost by the requirement for analog buffering of the signal. Nevertheless, it does have some uses and the domestic temperature control circuit of Chapter 9 is an example of one application.

A parallel output port can be used to drive a binary weighted resistor network such as shown in Figure 7-2, but limitations are imposed by the output impedance of the port and sensitivity to logic supply levels.

A/D CONVERTERS USING MICROCOMPUTERS

Figure 7-16 shows the basic method for implementing analog-to-digital conversion using a D/A converter, a comparator and a microcomputer. The A/D conversion logic is implemented in software by the microcomputer, and can be programmed to emulate either the successive-approximations or tracking methods discussed earlier. However, there are some important speed limitations incurred by using the microcomputer to carry-out the required logic.

Successive-approximations is primarily a high-speed A/D conversion technique, and it requires the analog input to be absolutely steady whilst a conversion is made if gross errors are not to occur. For this reason successive-approximation converters are often

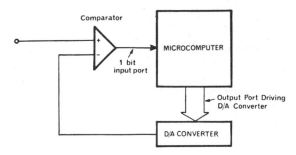

Figure 7-16. A/D converter using microcomputer to implement logic

preceded by a sample-and-hold circuit. Unfortunately, most microcomputer designs are not well-suited to carrying out the successive-approximations method and as a result conversion times are unduly long. This, in turn, places more stringent emphasis on the analog signal remaining steady over the whole conversion period, and therefore the use of a sample-and-hold circuit becomes more essential.

The tracking type of A/D converter is more suitable for software implementation because only a single instruction is required to increment a value. However, conversion times are inherently slow and this can lead to a loss in valuable software time. Nevertheless, in applications where the A/D conversion is used to monitor and follow a fairly low-frequency signal, the tracking method has much to recommend it.

In any A/D conversion process the microcomputer can, in principle, be used to replace the conversion logic. However, in practice, this is often not feasible because the conversion uses valuable software time which the microcomputer can ill afford. Also, many converters like successive-approximations require the undivided attention of the microcomputer during the conversion process and it is not always possible to mask-off all interrupts for a whole conversion period.

SUMMARY

This chapter has, of necessity, given a brief coverage of the type of D/A and A/D converters in common use. These are:

D/A — Weighted resistors
  — R-2R ladder
  — Pulse-width modulation

A/D — Tracking
  — Successive-approximation
  — Dual-slope integrating type
  — Charge-balancing
  — Voltage-to-frequency conversion
  — Multiple comparator.

The choice of conversion technique is governed by many factors and Chapter 8 attempts to show some of the design parameters that should be considered when using data converters.

Using A/D and D/A Converters with Microcomputers

Chapter 8

INTRODUCTION

Since the world in which we live is largely an analog one, virtually every computer has some form of interface circuit for converting signals from digital to analog form or vice-versa. This chapter is devoted to a discussion of the interface techniques used to connect analog and digital circuits to each other.

In using microcomputers, the complete system design is subject to many constraints. Three of these are:

(i)   The microcomputer operates at a speed dictated by its own clock frequency, and not by the sequence in which external events occur.

(ii)   Generally it is desirable to reduce the number of integrated-circuit packages and the number of connections, so as to reduce the overall cost and to improve system reliability.

(iii)   Microcomputers are relatively slow and, where possible, hardware should relieve the microcomputer of time consuming tasks.

These three key design parameters occur repeatedly in this and the succeeding chapter.

DIGITAL-TO-ANALOG CIRCUITS AND THE MICROCOMPUTER INTERFACE

One of the fundamental principles in using output devices with a microcomputer is that the output information is latched. The information, which the microcomputer sends to the output port, is placed in latches and retained until the microcomputer chooses to change the information at some later time. The microcomputer only addresses the output port at sporadic intervals and between these intervals the output device must be self-sustaining. Applying this principle to digital-to-analog converters, it can be seen that the ideal D/A converter should include a set of latches so as to hold the specified value until it is updated. However, this apparently simple requirement is not easily achieved because the technology for fabricating D/A converters and that for fabricating logic is not always the same, and therefore it is difficult to include the two on the same integrated circuit. One solution is to build D/A converters in hybrid form by mounting separate latch, switch and resistor circuits on a common substrate and interconnecting them, but this method is expensive. Fortunately, two monolithic techniques do lend themselves fairly well to single chip fabrication of D/A converters: these are I^2L logic, which is a form of logic using bipolar transistors and CMOS logic. I^2L technology has the advantage that high quality analog circuits and high speed logic can be included on the same chip. CMOS, on the other hand, is not suited to sophisticated analog circuits, but has the advantage of excellent analog switches, good logic capability and low power consumption. It should be noted that it is desirable to keep on-chip power dissipation low for D/A and A/D converters so as to minimise errors due to local heating of the R-2R ladder.

Clearly, the simple D/A converter is not quite as simple as it would appear. The microcomputer interface problem is compounded by the fact that most microcomputers to date are 8-bit machines, so that data can only be transmitted to output ports in 8-bit bytes. However, this only provides a bipolar accuracy of about 1% and this is inadequate for many analog applications. Consequently most D/A converters have either 10- or 12-bit resolution, and this requires that the output be transmitted as two consecutive data bytes. In doing this, the two bytes have to be re-assembled at the D/A converter as a single word and then presented to the ladder circuit. It is not appropriate to re-assemble the word using the latches directly connected to the D/A ladder switches because this would cause extreme glitches on the D/A output during the period when the transfer of the two data bytes is half completed. Thus in order to connect a 10- or 12-bit D/A converter to an 8-bit micro-computer, it is necessary to use the multiple latches method as shown in Figure 8-1. This arrangement is known as a double-buffered D/A.

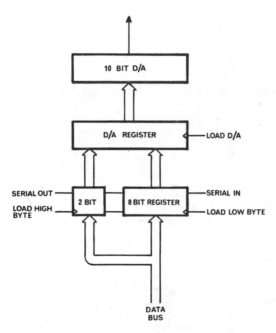

Figure 8-1. Double-buffered D/A converter (AD7522)

Separate clock inputs for the high and low byte latches are provided so that these can be strobed whenever the microcomputer sends information to them. A third clock input serves to load the latch set driving the D/A converter from the input latches, so that once a complete new word has been received it can be transferred "en bloc" to the main D/A circuit.

An alternative method of transferring information from a micro-computer to an output port is to do the data transfer in serial mode. Then only three interconnections are necessary: one line carries the output information, another provides the clock pulse for clocking the information into the output port which consists of a shift register, and a third loads the shift register into the D/A register. This method has the advantage that it requires only three pins to connect any number of output ports to the microcomputer, and since this number is so low, it is economically viable to completely isolate the analog output from the digital circuits by means of optical isolators.

For multiple output devices the serial output mode can be utilised either by connecting all the output devices in a long string as shown in Figure 8-2 and then shifting in new information as one long word, or by using a demultiplexer to supply the clock and having common data and D/A register load strobes as shown in Figure 8-3.

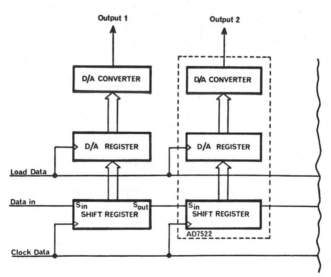

Figure 8-2. Loading multiple D/A converters in full serial mode

The circuit of Figure 8-2 has the disadvantage that a complete set of data has to be output each time one D/A converter is changed and the data transfer rate is consequently slow. With the circuit of Figure 8-3, data is shifted into the one device which is clocked from the demultiplexer, whilst all other devices remain unchanged thus allowing the overall data transfer rate to be higher. Since serial output to D/A converters uses few interconnections, it is possible to obtain much higher packing density of D/A converters on printed circuit boards. The serial data link technique is also an important factor with single chip microcomputers because it minimises pin count, reduces overall systems costs and increases reliability.

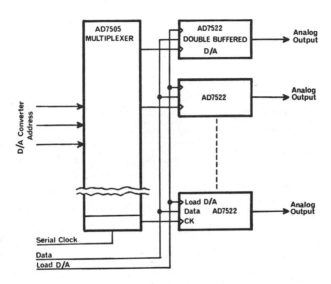

Figure 8-3. Loading multiple D/A converters in serial-parallel mode

MULTIPLE BYTE PARALLEL DATA TRANSFERS

The previous section referred to the fact that in order to parallel load a 10- or 12-bit D/A converter from an 8-bit microcomputer, the full word must be sent as two 8-bit bytes. The two bytes are re-assembled into a single word at the D/A converter. However, there are many ways in which 10 bits of information can be sent as two 8-bit bytes as shown below:

$$\text{Word to be transmitted} = b_9 b_8 b_7 b_6 b_5 b_4 b_3 b_2 b_1 b_0$$

First Byte — Address A000   Second Byte — Address A001

(a) $0\ 0\ 0\ 0\ 0\ 0\ b_9 b_8$ $b_7 b_6 b_5 b_4 b_3 b_2 b_1 b_0$

(b) $b_7 b_6 b_5 b_4 b_3 b_2 b_1 b_0$ $0\ 0\ 0\ 0\ 0\ 0\ b_9 b_8$

(c) $b_9 b_8 0\ 0\ 0\ 0\ 0\ 0$ $b_7 b_6 b_5 b_4 b_3 b_2 b_1 b_0$

(d) $b_7 b_6 b_5 b_4 b_3 b_2 b_1 b_0$ $b_9 b_8 0\ 0\ 0\ 0\ 0\ 0$

Figure 8-4 gives the connections to the AD7522 10-bit double-buffered D/A converter for two of these four cases.

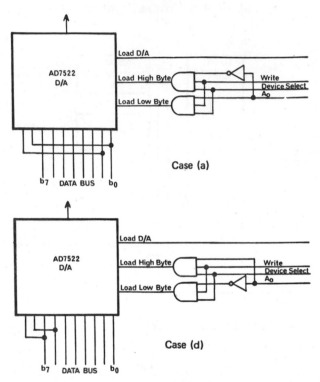

Figure 8-4. Multiple byte parallel loaded D/A converter

The various methods of transmitting multiple bytes arise as a result of the internal architecture of the microprocessor and the manner in which the data is generated and used within the microcomputer. Most 8-bit microprocessors have a single instruction which transfers a 16-bit data word as two 8-bit bytes. Unfortunately some transfer the data with the least significant byte first and others transfer the data with the most significant byte first — hence cases a and b above. In addition, some applications require the sign bit of the data (e.g., b_9) to be at the most significant end of the high data byte so that it can be easily shifted into the carry flag and examined with a "jump on carry" instruction — hence cases c and d.

FAST ANALOG-TO-DIGITAL CONVERTERS AND THE MICROCOMPUTER INTERFACE

All of the considerations discussed above also apply to A/D converters, but in addition, there is one other important system parameter — namely conversion time. The ideal A/D converter would yield a digital value immediately it is interrogated by the microcomputer. However, all A/D converters have a finite conversion time and this governs the way in which the converter can be used. Where the conversion time is short in relation to the instruction cycle time, the easiest method is to start the A/D conversion with one instruction, follow this by a number of dummy instructions (such as add zero to the accumulator) which allows time for the conversion to take place, and then read the result from the converter. Figure 8-5 shows the connections for connecting the AD7570 10-bit successive-approximations A/D converter to the Intel 8080 microprocessor. Address A000 (hex) is decoded and ANDed with the write signal, so that the instruction "Store accumulator A at A000 (hex)" is used to provide the

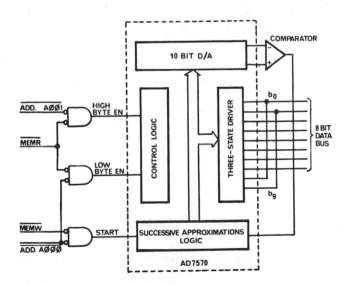

Figure 8-5. Successive-approximations converter connection to 8080 where dummy instructions are used to wait for the end of conversion

start signal. It does not matter that the microprocessor will attempt to write the accumulator contents into the A/D converter because the A/D converter will not accept them. The store instruction is followed by a number of "Clear accumulator" instructions which allow the AD7570 time to make the conversion, and finally the analog value is read from the A/D converter. An indirect addressing instruction is used to transfer the low order byte to the microprocessor, the index register is incremented to give address A001 and then the high order byte is transferred to the microprocessor where the two bytes are automatically assembled into a 16-bit word.

An alternative approach for using fast A/D converters with microcomputers is to connect the A/D converter so that the microprocessor sees it as a "slow memory." To start a conversion the microcomputer executes a read instruction at the address occupied by the A/D converter. This causes the converter to start conversion, and it issues a "busy" signal to the microcomputer. The microcomputer uses the busy signal to suspend operation until the signal disappears, whereupon the instruction cycle is resumed and the two bytes are transferred to the microprocessor as described above. The method of using the busy signal to temporarily halt the instruction cycle varies from one processor to another. Some (like the Intel 8080) insert dummy "do-nothing" sub-steps into the instruction cycle; others (like the National SC/MP) just stop and wait and some (like the Motorola 6800) stretch the microprocessor clock pulse. Unfortunately it is not always permissible to stretch the clock pulse sufficiently to use the method described above and it is important to check the microprocessor data sheet before using this technique. The "slow-memory" approach to A/D converter interface has the advantage that it uses a minimum of instructions and the value is returned to the microprocessor in the shortest possible time. The connections for using the AD7570 10-bit converter with an Intel 8080 are shown in Figure 8-6.

SLOW A/D CONVERTERS AND THE MICROCOMPUTER INTERFACE

If the methods described above for fast A/D converters are used with slow converters, then valuable computing time is lost whilst

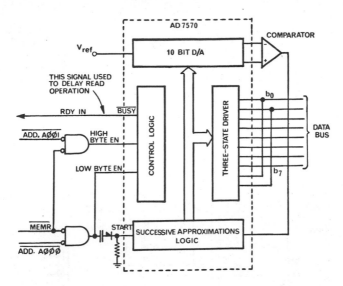

Figure 8-6. Using a successive-approximations converter as slow memory (connections shown for 8080)

the microcomputer waits for the digital value to become available. Therefore it is better to interface a slow A/D converter to the microcomputer so that, once the microprocessor has initiated the A/D conversion process, it can return to the main-line program to do other calculations until the conversion is complete. This is achieved by connecting the A/D converter so as to behave as an interrupting input device. Figure 8-7 shows the AD7550 quad-slope converter (see Chapter 7) connected to operate in this way: all outputs of the AD7550 are three-state logic. The busy line of the converter is connected as an interrupt to the microcomputer so that, when a conversion is complete, the converter interrupts the microprocessor and causes a jump to the A/D handling routine. As long as the converter is idle and has a digital value available at its output, the busy line will attempt to cause an interrupt. It is therefore necessary to use the microcomputer to mask-off the converter interrupt so that an interrupt is only permitted at the completion of a conversion. The program flow-chart is then as shown in Figure 8-8. Many of the present microcomputers do not have the facility for selectively masking-off the I/O devices and it may be necessary to build an interrupt mask in hardware as shown in the dotted portion of Figure 8-7. The interrupt latch is set on completion of the A/D conversion and is reset when the last byte is read from the converter.

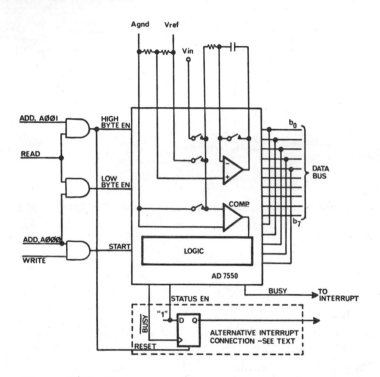

Figure 8-7. Connections for using an integrating A/D converter as an interrupting input device

It is of course possible to use the A/D converter with any of the I/O techniques described in Chapter 3. Program-controlled I/O is often used because it does not require a sophisticated interrupt structure and can be implemented with the minimum of extra hardware. Figure 8-9 shows the AD7550 connected for program-controlled I/O. Note that the two status lines "over-range" and "busy" are connected to the three-state data bus in the MSB and LSB positions so that they can easily be interrogated by reading the status word to the microprocessor accumulator and then shifting them into the carry flag.

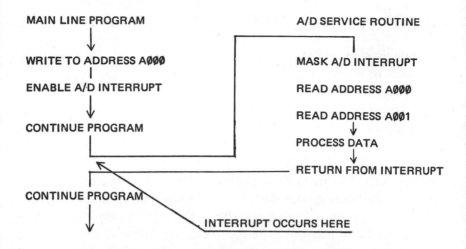

Figure 8-8. Program flow for handling interrupting A/D converter

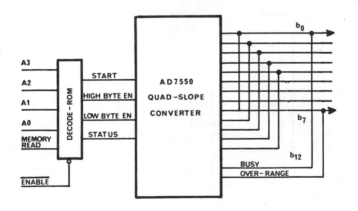

Figure 8-9. Integrating converter connected for program controlled I/O

Most microcomputers which have analog interface elements also include a real-time clock so as to control the rate at which the analog environment is addressed by the microcomputer. It is a relatively simple matter to include the reading and restart of the A/D converter as part of the real-time clock handling routine provided that the A/D conversion time is slightly less than the real-time clock frequency.

MAKING A/D CONVERTERS APPEAR AS MEMORY

It was stated earlier that the ideal A/D should immediately respond to a read signal. This is not feasible for many reasons, but nevertheless there are many applications which require the A/D to have the most current value always available to the microprocessor. In this case the software is not constrained by the A/D conversion process and the A/D converter appears to the microprocessor as memory. For most A/D converters it is possible to achieve this requirement by inserting a buffer register between the converter and the microcomputer buses. The timing should be arranged so that the register is loaded by the A/D during a period when the microprocessor will not attempt a read operation — for example, whilst the program counter is being incremented. Figure 8-10 shows the AD7550 connected for this type of application.

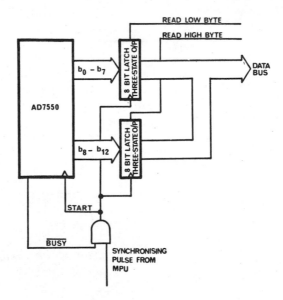

Figure 8-10. Continuously running A/D converter connected to appear to the MPU as memory

The buffer memory approach to A/D interfaces can be used to advantage to construct multi-channel A/D converters as shown in Figure 8-11. The A/D converter consists of a counter whose output feeds a D/A converter. The D/A output is compared with the input signals and, at the point where the input and the D/A value are equal, the counter contents are written into the memory location associated with that particular comparator. The memory is a multi-port device which can be written into one address and read from another at the same time (e.g., SN74170). Clock pulses are continuously fed to the counter so that it scans through the whole range of analog values and repeatedly updates the memory contents. To obtain the analog value of an input channel the microcomputer simply addresses the memory. To avoid reading whilst writing, memory updates should take place at points when the microcomputer will not access memory. Note that this is a form of memory shared DMA as discussed at the end of Chapter 3.

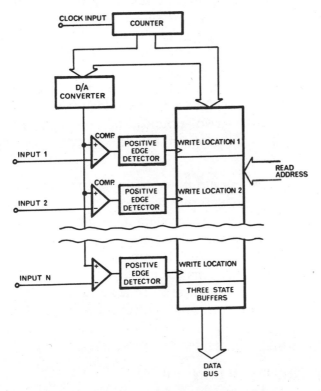

Figure 8-11. Memory shared DMA A/D converter

ANALOG CIRCUITS IN A DIGITAL ENVIRONMENT

The function of this small section is to offer some guidelines for connecting analog peripherals into a microcomputer system so as to reduce noise problems and aid system checks. There are three major noise sources in a microcomputer, namely high frequency clocks, noise on the power supply connections and noise generated by the power supply. Clock noises are best excluded by enclosing the analog circuits within a shield; hybrid and encapsulated converters often have this feature as standard. Where switching regulators are used to obtain the power supplies, the regulator itself should be enclosed in a shield and analog circuits should be as far away from the regulator as possible. Twisted pair wiring of analog signal lines helps to reduce magnetic coupling. Ground loops should be avoided at all costs and a strict ground current management procedure should be followed. Analog signals should not have long signal paths, nor should they run close to digital lines. Where possible, analog lines should be surrounded by ground with a ground plane on the opposite side of the board: this minimises stray capacitance and reduces the risk of coupling from other signals. If the supplies to the analog circuits are derived from the +5V logic supplies, a dc-to-dc converter which gives excellent isolation between the two grounds and rejects high frequency noise that may be present on the +5V supply line should be chosen.

Microcomputer systems are notoriously difficult to check and all designs should include some features which help the service engineer to trouble-shoot the system. One simple arrangement for checking the A/D function is to have an input signal multiplexer which has inputs connected to ground and $V_{REF/2}$. A small resident ROM uses the microcomputer to switch in the various inputs, exercise the A/D and present the results so that the function and calibration can be observed. Of course where a D/A converter is also present in the system, it can be used to provide the A/D input and thereby generate an overall system accuracy check.

FUTURE TRENDS IN CONVERTERS

At the beginning of this chapter three design criteria were given

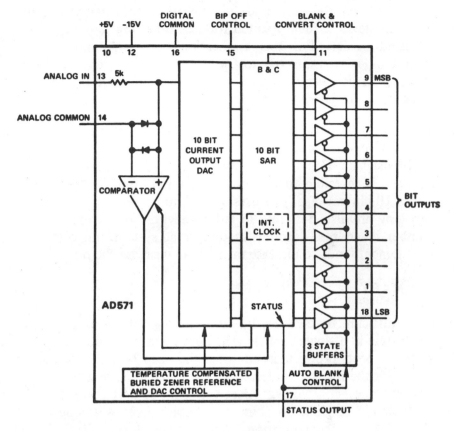

Figure 8-12. Minimum package size A/D converter

and, of those three, the most difficult one for the converter designer to meet is minimum package size. The number of pins available to an integrated circuit designer has always been a limitation, but with analog-to-digital circuits the problem is compounded by the necessity for separate analog and digital power and ground lines, and the large number of signal paths associated with analog circuits. As a result, there is a trend towards including more and more analog functions directly on the integrated-circuit. Figure 8-12 shows the AD571 successive-approximations converter which is built using I^2L technology. It has been possible to accommodate the complete A/D function into an 18-pin dual in-line package by including all functions such as voltage reference, clock and comparator on the chip and by using minimum digital control pins. The device is ideally suited for use in the slow memory mode discussed earlier. For this application the blank and convert control input is connected to the read signal from the computer and the status output is used to put the processor in the wait mode until conversion is complete.

Another method of reducing pin count is to multiplex digital information onto a common bus and to use carefully encoded control signals. For example, by using careful design techniques it might be possible to build a 10-bit serial input D/A converter into a 10-pin package. Features such as improved on-chip address decoding are also desirable in future devices so as to reduce the number of address decoders in the overall system, but often this requirement tends to increase rather than decrease the pin count.

SUMMARY

It is difficult to completely cover analog interfaces to micro-computers in a single chapter. The above text has concentrated on system aspects rather than circuit design, and for full coverage of the latter the reader is referred to the companion text "Analog — Digital Conversion Notes." Also, the text has only considered the interface of single converters, and topics such as analog multi-plexers and data acquisition systems have been omitted. These topics are an extension of the discussion to date and the reader should not have difficulty in extending the concepts given above to these cases. The importance of careful circuit layout cannot be overemphasised. A 2.5V change in 10 nanoseconds will couple a 25 millivolt spike to a 100 ohm impedance through only 1 pico-farad. A 12-bit converter with 5 volts full-scale has a resolution of 1.2 mV, so that a spike as generated above would cause an error of 21 bits.

Applications of Microprocessors

Chapter 9

INTRODUCTION

Before designing a microprocessor system it is necessary to examine the application in the light of certain critical parameters. These include:

(i)   The number of input and output ports required
(ii)   Input/output structures and interrupts
(iii)   Speed of operation
(iv)   Production and development costs
(v)   Previous experience
(vi)   Existing hardware and designs.

None of the parameters listed above can be considered in isolation and their relative importance changes from one application to another. For small production runs, the overall development cost is a significant portion of the net selling price and under such circumstances it is probably best to capitalise on previous experience and existing hardware. This often results in using a much more powerful microprocessor than is necessary but nevertheless results in a considerable reduction in development costs. By contrast, in a high-volume application, development costs can be offset against a much longer production run and the first consideration in choosing a microprocessor becomes production cost. This is usually closely related to the number of components used in the design, and as a result microprocessor systems which are to be produced in quantity are designed to keep the package count to a minimum.

The conflict between high-performance general-purpose processors and low-cost minimum package count systems has produced five basic categories of processor systems:

(i)　High-performance minicomputer-type processors (e.g., 9900, CP1600)

(ii)　High-performance 8-bit general-purpose processors (e.g., 8080, 6800, 2650)

(iii)　Low-cost general-purpose processors (e.g., SC/MP)

(iv)　High-performance dedicated processors (e.g., PPS 8/2)

(v)　Low-cost dedicated processors (e.g., F8, ALPS)

Table 9-1 gives a rough indication of the normal size of these five categories. The cheaper devices tend to trade off high-speed and powerful instruction sets in return for features such as on-chip input-output ports, built-in system clock and on-chip RAM.

Table 9-1. Microprocessor Types and System Size

	TYPICAL DEVICE TYPES	MOST COMFORTABLE ADDRESS CAPABILITY (KILOWORDS)	NUMBER OF PACKAGES IN A SYSTEM
Minicomputer type	9900, CP1600	4 to 64	20 to 100
High-performance 8-bit general-purpose	8080, 6800	2 to 32	10 to 50
Low-cost general-purpose	SC/MP, 4040	up to 2	3 to 10
High-performance dedicated processors	9002, PPS8/2	up to 4	2 to 10
Low-cost dedicated processors	F8, ALPS	up to 4	1 to 4

This chapter illustrates aspects of microcomputer system design by means of five case studies. These cover the full spectrum of applications from replacement of analog and digital circuits up to dedicated minicomputer systems. Each case study gives details of the application, method of operation and factors which influenced the overall system design.

STAR DRUM PRINTER INTERFACE

The application. This section deals with a circuit used to drive a STAR drum printer from an Intel 8080 microprocessor. In the complete application the drum printer is the output device of an intelligent instrument, but the text here is restricted to the printer drive circuit alone.

The printer consists of a rotating drum which has characters embossed on its surface. The characters are arranged as 16 columns with 13 characters in each column. To print a character a hammer briefly forces the paper against the drum so that it picks up the appropriate character from the rotating drum. There are 16 hammers, one per column, and the drive circuit is required to activate each hammer at the correct instant of time so that the desired character is printed. The drive circuit also starts the drum motor whenever a print-out is to take place, and provides a paper feed after printing each row of characters.

Two timing signals are provided by the printer for use by the interface circuit. These are a reset signal, which gives a positive going pulse each time the rotating drum begins a revolution, and a character timing signal which gives a short pulse of between 200 and 400μs at the start and finish of each character. Figure 9-1 shows the timing diagram. The timing signals are generated by electromagnetic pick-ups and need some amplification. Paper feed is achieved by activating the paper-feed electromagnet for a minimum of 15ms. When starting the motor, 200ms should be allowed for the motor to run up to full speed before printing begins.

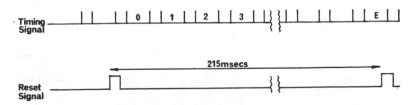

Figure 9-1. Printer timing diagram

The circuit. Figure 9-2 shows the block diagram of the circuit used. It consists of two 8212 8-bit latched output ports which are used to drive the 16 hammers, a 2-bit output port which drives the motor and the paper-feed mechanism, and a 2-bit input port which is used to connect the reset and character timing pulses onto the data bus. A dual 2-line to 4-line decoder is connected to the address bus so that the ports are allocated the following addresses:

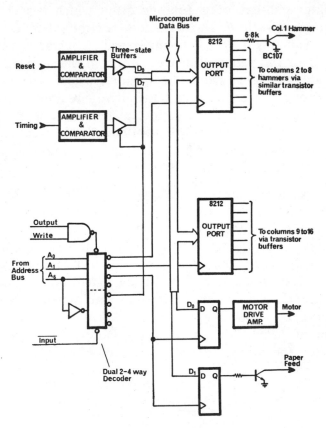

Figure 9-2. "STAR" printer interface circuit

Output Address   x1xxxx00   Port for column hammers 1 to 8
D_0 corresponds to column 1
D_7 corresponds to column 8

Output Address	x1xxxx01	Port for column hammers 9 to 16 D_0 corresponds to column 9 D_7 corresponds to column 16
Output Address	x1xxxx10	D_0 port switches on drum motor D_1 port drives paper-feed mechanism
Input Address	x1xxxx00	D_0 input port – Reset pulses D_7 input port – Character pulses

(x in the address indicates undefined bit)

The Intel 8080 has separate input and output instructions and when these are executed the input (or output) control line is strobed and the appropriate 8-bit port address is encoded into bits A_0 to A_7 on the address bus. The output strobe line is ANDed with the write pulse to provide an enable input to the address decoder, and the decoder output provides the clock pulse for writing information from the system data bus into the output port latches. Similarly the inputs from the two magnetic pick-up amplifiers are placed on the system data bus when the appropriate address and the input enable line are valid.

The circuit operates by putting a logic 1 on the appropriate output bit at the correct instant of time so as to print the desired character. The timing is done entirely by software. The timing pulses from the magnetic pick-up are polled using an input instruction; hardware interrupt is not used.

The software. Sixteen adjacent memory locations are used to store, in binary code, the 16 characters to be printed. When the drum has character "0" available for printing, the software makes a scan through the 16 locations to see if any of the characters is a zero; for those that are zero a logic "1" is sent to the appropriate hammer and then, after the specified period, all outputs are returned to logic "0." The process is repeated for character "1" and so on until one revolution has been completed. Then the paper feed is activated and the drum motor switched off.

The Intel 8080 has a number of internal registers as shown in Figure 9-3, and these can be used either as single 8-bit registers or two may be paired together for use as a 16-bit address pointer. In this application the internal registers are allocated as follows:

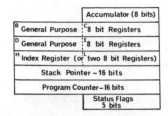

Figure 9-3. Internal organisation of Intel 8080

A   — Accumulator.

B   — Working register.

C   — Hammer control bit pattern. The contents of C are eventually sent to the output port to turn on the appropriate hammers.

D   — Counter to count the number of characters scanned through in the 16 memory locations.

E   — Counts character pulses and thereby gives an indication of current character available for printing.

H and L — Used as a 16-bit address pointer to point to characters stored in memory.

The printer software routine is called as a subroutine and the main program arranges for the 16 characters printed to be in the locations pointed to by H and L. Upon entering the print routine, the program turns on the motor by sending a logic "1" to the motor drive output port and then waits until it has received 2 reset pulses before scanning through the first 8 characters to see if any is a zero. The software determines which characters are "O" and builds up a hammer drive pattern for the output port for columns 1 to 8 in register C.

The contents of register C are then sent to the output port and the routine is repeated for columns 9 to 16. The scan and output routine is done quite fast so that the delay between loading the two hammer ports is not significant to the electromechanical printer. The software now waits until a character pulse signifying the end of a character is received and the two ports are then loaded with all zeros. The process is repeated for the 1's character, 2's character, etc. Finally after the thirteenth character is printed, the paper-feed mechanism is activated for two character pulses and the motor is turned off.

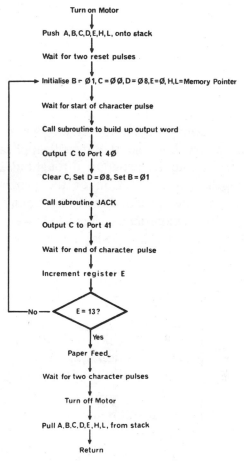

Figure 9-4a. "STAR" printer interface program flow chart

Figure 9-4a shows the complete program flow-chart. Subroutine "JACK" (see Figure 9-4b) performs the scan through 8 consecutive memory locations and builds up the hammer drive pattern in register C.

Software techniques. The program makes great use of the internal registers of the 8080 to store loop counts and bit patterns. Since most of the instructions which manipulate the internal registers are single byte instructions, the total program is economical in program storage (about 110 bytes). The instructions OR, SHIFT and COMPARE are used to advantage: in a simpler processor without say the "COMPARE" instruction, the program length and execution time would be somewhat longer. In this particular application, the printer is used at the end of a long data analysis routine and there is no possibility of an interrupt occurring, but where an interrupt might occur it would be necessary to either mask-off the interrupt or rewrite the subroutine as a re-entrant one. This particular program was written in assembly language run on an Intellec 80 development system. The assembly language facility was necessary because the overall application was large and it was not feasible to program throughout in hexadecimal code, although the printer section of the program could have easily been written in hexadecimal code. The total system development time taken by an experienced 8080 user was about 40 hours. This included the time required to lay out and construct a printed circuit board.

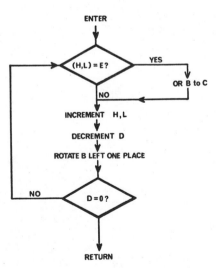

Figure 9-4b. Subroutine to build up output hammer drive 8-bit word

AN INTELLIGENT LAMP-DIMMER FOR STUDIO LIGHTING

<u>The application.</u> This application is the control of the intensity of

individual studio lights. It is required to set the lamp intensity from a master control computer and to fade lamp intensities from one setting to another over a specified period of time. Each lamp intensity during the fade time can be expressed by the equation:

$$\text{Lamp Intensity} = \left[\frac{\text{new}}{\text{setting}} - \frac{\text{old}}{\text{setting}}\right].\frac{t}{\text{fade time}} + \text{old setting}$$

$$= (\text{new} - \text{old})\frac{t}{\tau} + \text{old}$$

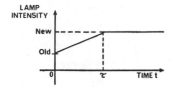

Figure 9-5. Lamp fading method

The lamp intensity setting and the fade time are sent from the master computer to the lamp dimmer as two 8-bit bytes: the intensity setting has a 0 as its most significant bit and the fade time has a 1 as its most significant bit. It is the function of the lamp dimmer to accept the two 8-bit words and solve the above equation for its own particular lamp. The circuit also handles phase control of the triac used to dim the lamp.

In a typical application the master computer handles between 100 and 200 lamps so that the task of continuously solving the above equation for each of the lamps is a particularly onerous one. In the approach discussed here, the equation solving is delegated to each dimmer circuit and the master computer becomes simple enough to be replaced by a general-purpose 8-bit microprocessor. The design of the complete system is outside the scope of this chapter and the text concentrates only on the intelligent lamp dimmer. The microprocessor-based dimmer replaces a D/A converter and an analog phase-control firing circuit, as well as relieving the master computer of some of its workload.

Lamp dimmer circuit and the principle of operation. Figure 9-6. shows the complete dimmer circuit. Information is sent from the master computer as two 8-bit bytes. The two bytes are transmitted at least one full mains cycle apart so as to give the circuit time to read in each byte. The fade period begins 8 cycles after receiving the new intensity information.

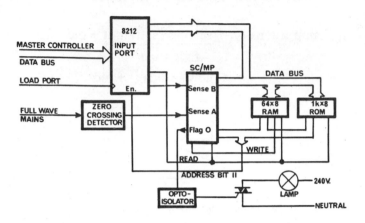

Figure 9-6. Block diagram of fading circuit

One of the features of the SC/MP microprocessor is that it has simple on-chip input and output ports which are used to advantage in this application. The inputs consist of an interrupt (Sense A), a single bit input (Sense B) and a serial input. There are 3 output flags (F_0, F_1 and F_2) and a serial output.

A mains-driven zero-crossing detector drives the interrupt line and the input request flag contained within the 8212 is connected to the Sense B input. When new information is written into the input port, the input request flag is automatically set and this can be detected by the processor. Output flag F_0 is connected through an opto-isolator to drive the triac. Phase-control of the triac is achieved by sensing the start of a mains cycle and waiting for a known number of clock cycles before firing the triac.

The 8-bit byte from the master computer gives scope for 128 different intensity and 128 fade time settings. One unit of a fade-time is taken as 8 full main cycles, which gives maximum fade times of 20.32 and 16.9 secs at 50 and 60Hz respectively. The relationship between lamp intensity and number of cycles delay is not a linear one and this nonlinearity is accommodated by a 127-word look-up table. The desired lamp intensity expressed as a binary integer between 0 and 127 is used to form an address to reference the look-up table and obtain the appropriate delay time.

Techniques. The SC/MP has a limited instruction set and, in addition, an average instruction execution time of 30μs. These two factors combine to produce an 8-bit multiplication time of about 5ms and an 8-bit division time of 8ms. Clearly it is not feasible to evaluate the fading equation for each half cycle and alternative methods must be used. The technique employed is to evaluate the following expression in the eight cycles preceding the start of the actual fade time.

$$\text{Step size per unit of fade time} = \frac{(\text{new} - \text{old})}{\tau}$$

Thereafter the intensity is increased by one step size for every eight mains cycles until the fade time is completed. The final result is checked with the desired final value to eliminate errors resulting from round-off in the division process.

Whilst the microprocessor is counting out the delay prior to firing the triac, it is unable to make any useful calculations. In the case of the 8-cycle lead-in to a fade period, this could cause problems when the delay time is long because there would not be enough time left in the mains half-cycle to do the necessary calculations. To overcome this the microprocessor checks the delay time in the preceding half cycle, and if the firing point is in the first $\frac{\pi}{2}$ radians, it sets the interrupt vector so that, on receipt of the interrupt, the processor times out the delay and then does the calculations. If the firing point is in the range $\frac{\pi}{2}$ to π radians, a different interrupt vector is loaded into the vector register so that the processor does the calculations, adjusts the delay time to compensate for the time taken to do the calculations and then times out the modified delay before firing the triac. It will be observed that the ability of the SC/MP to dynamically change the interrupt vector is a particularly useful feature.

The main reasons for selecting the SC/MP microprocessor for this application were low cost, 8-bit compatibility with the master computer, on-chip output for driving the triac, interrupt capability and the ability to use UV erasable ROM's for program storage without any support circuits. A total production run of only 250 units was anticipated and mask-programmed ROM's were not economically feasible.

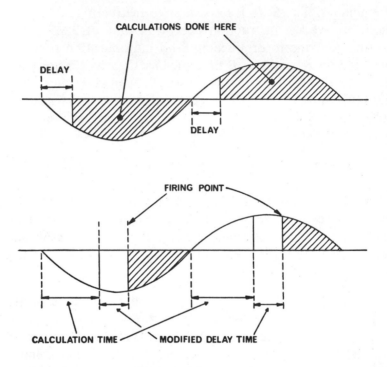

Figure 9-7. Diagrams illustrating relationship between triac firing point and period allocated to making calculations

System development was carried out by programming the U.V. erasable ROM's first with a simple program to check the hardware, and then with segments of the main program until the complete program was proved. Prior to designing the system, the SC/MP processor had been evaluated using a low-cost kit available from National Semiconductor. The task of writing the program and then converting to hexadecimal code for use by the programmer was done entirely by hand. This approach appears to be feasible for programs up to about 1 kbyte.

AN OPTICALLY ISOLATED THREE-TERM CONTROLLER

The application. A three-term controller is used in control systems to improve the overall response, stability, and accuracy of the control system. The controller has an input-output relationship as follows:

$$V_{out} = A.V._{in} + B \int V_{in}.dt + C.\frac{dV_{in}}{dt}$$

The application discussed here is a self-calibrating system in which the multiplying factors A, B and C are entered from a remote computer. Figure 9-8 shows the complete system diagram. The input voltage is converted into digital format using a V/F type A/D converter. This digital value is passed to the microcomputer which evaluates the equation and gives an analog output using a D/A converter. One important feature of the system is that the analog circuits are isolated from the digital section by means of five opto-isolators. This eliminates noise problems and, since all the analog circuits are low power devices, their supply voltages are derived from a small dc-to-dc converter.

The circuit. A V/F converter is used to generate a frequency proportional to the input voltage. This frequency is fed through an opto-isolator to a 12-bit counter whose contents are automatically loaded to a 12-bit latch every 80ms (once every four mains cycles at 50Hz) by a real-time clock. The real-time clock also drives the interrupt line of the microprocessor. Each interrupt causes the microprocessor to reset the counter and read the contents of the latch, so that the counter contents are proportional to the average input analog value over the 80ms period. A time frame of 80ms was chosen because it guarantees good normal mode rejection. The voltage-to-frequency converter is run with a frequency offset at 25.6KHz so that it can accommodate both positive and negative input voltages. Zero input voltage gives a frequency of 25.6KHz, negative input voltages decrease the frequency and positive inputs increase the frequency. Full-scale input of +2 volts gives 51.2KHz.

To obtain the true numerical value of the input the microprocessor subtracts the 80ms count for zero input volts from the 80ms count for the unknown input. An analog multiplexer is used at the

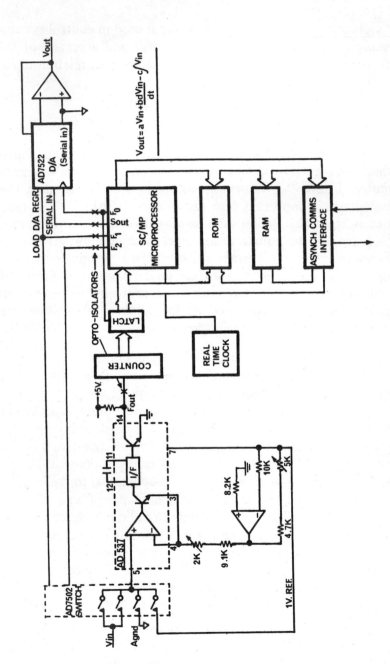

Figure 9-8. Optically isolated three-term controller

input to the V/F converter so that analog ground and the 1-volt internal reference of the V/F can be converted and used by the microcomputer to measure the frequency offset and check the calibration.

After the equation has been evaluated, the result is output to an AD7522 D/A converter using the serial mode of operation (see Chapter 8). Serial data transfer was used because it requires very few opto-isolators.

The circuit also includes a serial asynchronous communications interface for entering the factors A, B and C. In theory, it is possible to do the asynchronous communications using the serial input-output features of the microprocessor, but since the SC/MP is already overloaded with other software tasks, communications management was delegated to the separate device.

Software techniques. Voltage-to-frequency conversion was chosen for the conversion method not only because of the optical coupling facility but also because the true integral of the input signal can be obtained by adding successive data samples. This significantly reduces the software. The differential of the input signal is calculated using the least squares moving point polynomial*

$$\frac{dx_n}{dt} = \frac{-2x_{n-2} - x_{n-1} + x_{n+1} + 2x_{n+2}}{10}$$

where x_n is the sample value at time n. Most of the software time is taken up in multiplying in the factors A, B and C. All the arithmetic is done in 16-bit fixed point two's complement notation. 16-bit precision is not necessary for the application but it does provide a fairly straightforward way of avoiding round-off and overflow errors.

Summary. One of the disadvantages of the circuit discussed here is that it is only suitable for low speed control systems, the data sample rate is only 12.5Hz. The speed limitation is imposed by two factors; first, the V/F conversion technique is inherently slow, and second, the SC/MP microprocessor is slow and has a limited

---

*See Savitzky and Golay, Smoothing and Differentiation of Data by Simplified Least Squares Procedures, Analytical Chemistry, Vol. 36 No. 8, July 1969, pp. 1627–1639.

instruction set. The authors have used the SC/MP microprocessor in several applications and it has been found that the on-chip input and output features are extremely powerful, but the absence of direct addressing instructions and automatic stack management make it difficult to program. Another disadvantage is that all internal register manipulations are made using the accumulator and this means that the accumulator cannot be used to temporarily store data. This in turn slows down program execution. Nevertheless, for slow, simple, low cost applications the SC/MP microprocessor has much to recommend it.

A DIGITAL CONTROLLER FOR A DOMESTIC HEATING SYSTEM

The application. A microprocessor system is required to replace the conventional electro-mechanical logic (bimetalic thermostat, time switches, etc.) associated with the control of the start-up/shut-down of the heating system and with the regulation of the temperature within the building. The controller is also to act as a digital clock and provide a display in hours and minutes. The heating system is switched on or off via a mains contactor with a low voltage coil and the temperature inside the building is monitored using a single-point temperature measurement (θ). The start-up time (t_s), the shut-down time (t_f) and the desired setting for the inside temperature (θ_D) are to be defined by the user after the controller has been installed. A typical inside temperature profile is shown in Figure 9-9. Simple ON/OFF control is acceptable for regulation of the inside temperature when the building is occupied. Outside the occupancy period, the heating system is to be switched off. The complete control system is to be mass-produced and should have low material and production costs.

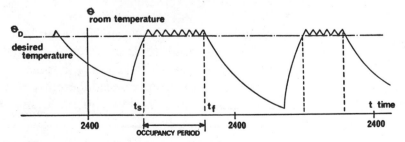

Figure 9-9. Typical inside temperature profile

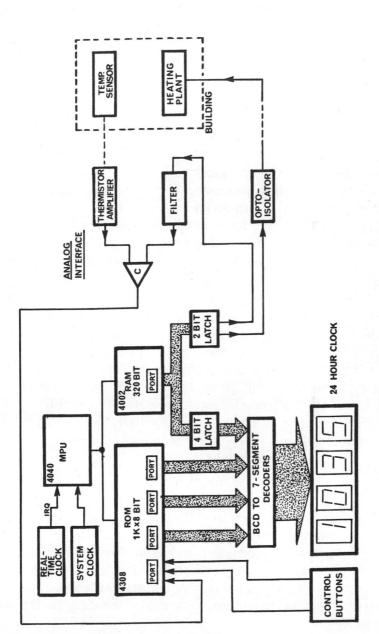

Figure 9-10. Production design of the heating controller

The design of the microprocessor-based controller. Since 4-bit resolution provides sufficient accuracy for domestic control applications, a cheap, but powerful, 4-bit microprocessor system is most appropriate. A design for the production version of the control system, based on the Intel 4040 chip, is shown in Figure 9-10. The main aim of the design is to minimise the number and complexity of the support circuits by using the microprocessor program to perform as many of the tasks associated with the control system as possible.

A single mask-programmed ROM chip holds the entire program and a single RAM chip provides sufficient data storage for this application. (The microprocessor chip itself includes a 96-bit scratch-pad memory.) Both ROM and RAM chips contain on-chip I/O ports which are used to drive the 24-hour clock display and to communicate with the other I/O devices.

The need for a costly analog interface is avoided by performing the logical operations associated with the analog-to-digital conversion in software and by using a minimum of external components. The techniques of the tracking A/D converter and the variable pulse-width D/A converter are most suitable for software realisation. By measuring the temperature with a thermistor sensor, the only external analog circuits are a thermistor amplifier, an analog filter and a voltage comparator. All can be constructed using low-cost integrated-circuit operational amplifiers. The desired temperature is set by adjusting the offset voltage of the thermistor amplifier.

Program execution is synchronised to real-time by interrupts generated at each zero-crossing of the mains voltage. A four-digit seven-segment display indicates the current time based on a 24-hour clock implemented in software. The clock display is also used in association with two push-button controls to allow the user to enter the desired start and stop times. Under program control one button causes the displayed time to be held or to be incremented at high speed. The other button enters the currently displayed value of time into a particular location in the data memory.

The coil of the mains contactor is driven through an opto-isolator to eliminate the effect of switching noise.

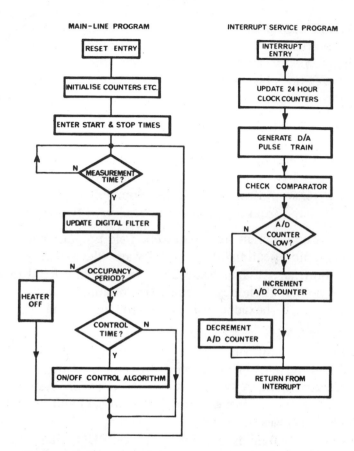

Figure 9-11. Simplifed program flow chart for heating controller

A simplified flow-chart for the program is shown in Figure 9-11. When power is first applied to the system, program execution starts at the reset entry point. The working registers and counters are initialised and the user enters the desired start-up and shut-down times using the control buttons. Interrupts are then enabled and real-time operation begins. The 24-hour clock counters are updated and the analog-to-digital conversion algorithms are processed in the interrupt service program which is entered every 10ms. All input-output data transfers are made under program control via the I/O ports. The output from the software A/D converter is sampled every minute and digitally filtered to reduce signal and conversion noise. The filtering algorithm involves the most complex of the arithmetic operations — an 8-bit x 4-bit unsigned binary multiplication. During the occupancy period, control action is taken at 5-minute time intervals.

The entire program has an approximate length of some 640 bytes.

System development techniques. Since the major part of the program was concerned with special-purpose input-output operations, it was essential to develop the software on a microprocessor system which was, in design, as near as possible to the final production version. However, the development version of the controller differed from the production version in two ways:

(i)   The program store had to be field-programmable to allow program modification during software development. In this application, an erasable RePROM and a Pseudo-ROM (a plug-in, ROM pin-compatible device consisting of a non-volatile read/write memory with hexadecimal keyboard input and hexadecimal display output) were used.

(ii)   A control panel was included in the system to allow user control of system operation and program execution during software development. A simple panel with the basic system controls (reset, stop, etc.), binary input (bit switches) and binary output (LED display) was sufficient.

Where the program is developed in RePROM, there are several techniques which may help to reduce the number of reprogramming operations and simplify the task of program debugging:

(i)   Groups of "no operation" instructions (op-code "00" hexadecimal) can be included at strategic points in the program so that jump instructions can be inserted at some future time to modify the program without erasing the RePROM.

(ii)   A short execution control program loaded at the reset start address of the RePROM allows the user to enter a desired program start address from the control panel and then to transfer program control to this address. Thus, several small programs can be loaded and tested in the same RePROM in one operation.

(iii)   The halt instruction and the stop/start control button allow the user to introduce temporary pauses in program execution at strategic points so that the status of I/O signals can be tested.

A program of this length and complexity can be written in machine code mnemonics and converted to hexadecimal code by hand. However, the task is tedious and detailed up-to-date program listings are essential if trivial syntax errors are to be avoided.

AN "INTELLIGENT" INSTRUMENT FOR MEASURING PERIPHERAL BLOOD FLOWRATES

The application. A microprocessor-based instrument is required to automate the radio-isotope clearance method of measuring peripheral blood flow in a tissue. A radio-active tracer is placed on the tissue and its rate of removal, as indicated by the radio-active decay curve, can be related to the blood flowrate through the tissue. For a single blood flow path through the tissue, the decay curve is exponential and the blood flowrate is evaluated from the "half-time" of the decay curve ($T_{1/2}$). Where more than one blood flow path exists, the curve will have several components, each with its own $T_{1/2}$ value. In this application the instrument is required to calculate two $T_{1/2}$ values defining the blood flowrates associated with two blood flow paths from a tissue.

The radio-activity level is monitored with a scintillation detector placed in contact with the tissue. Count rates are in the range 100 to 1000 pulses/sec. The instrument has two operating modes:

    (i)   A single sample mode to allow the operator to take spot readings of radio-activity and to measure and enter the "background" count rate.

    (ii)   A run mode to allow the operator to initiate the automatic collection and storage of a predefined number of radio-activity samples at a predefined sampling rate. From the collected data, the two $T_{1/2}$-values are then estimated using a simple numerical procedure based on the linear least-squares method.

During sampling, the last measured value of the count rate is to be displayed in integer format, and after estimation, the two $T_{1/2}$ values are displayed in four digit "movable" point format.

Figure 9-12 shows a typical decay curve and illustrates the required front panel controls and displays for the instrument.

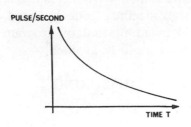

Figure 9-12a. Typical decay curve of radioactivity

Figure 9-12b. Blood flow-meter front panel.

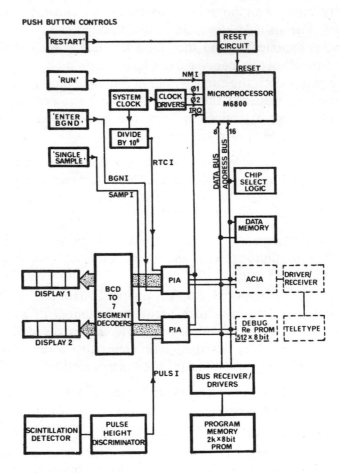

Figure 9-13. System design of blood flowmeter

The design of the microprocessor-based instrument. The instrument design is based on the Motorola M6800 microprocessor system. Extensive use is made of the microprocessor's powerful interrupt system and, to simplify the external circuits, I/O signals are connected into the microprocessor via general-purpose interface chips. As shown in Figure 9-13, the two 4-digit 7-segment displays are driven via decoders from two PIA (peripheral interface adapter) chips with each chip acting as a 16-bit parallel output port. The high priority "restart" and "run" front panel control buttons are connected directly to the microprocessor chip and generate the reset and non-maskable interrupt (NMI) signals respectively. The other control buttons, namely the "single sample" and "enter background" controls, are connected through a PIA to generate the SAMPI and BGNDI maskable interrupt signals respectively. The system clock, when divided down to 1Hz, generates the RTCI interrupt signal. The output from the scintillation detector, after passing through a pre-amplifier and pulse-height discriminator to reduce the background noise level, generates the PULSI interrupt signal. The PIA interrupt control logic allows each of the four types of maskable interrupt signals to be enabled or disabled individually under program control. The teletype, which is used only during program development, is connected into the system via an ACIA (asynchronous communications interface adapter) chip.

A single RAM chip provides sufficient memory capacity to satisfy the requirements of the program stack, the common working registers used by the extended-precision arithmetic routines, and the storage buffer for the count rate samples. The main program memory, which uses fusible-link PROM, is built on a separate board with signals interconnected to the microprocessor through three-state driver/receivers. During program development, a single RePROM chip, which holds the teletype paper-tape utilities and the software debug package, is also included in the system.

The application program can be divided into two main sections:

(i)   Interrupt servicing and control.
(ii)   Data analysis.

The interrupt control software synchronises the program execution with real-time, determines the mode of operation of the instrument and provides a measure of the count rate. For example, the count rate is determined by counting the number of PULSI interrupts occurring within a period of time defined by counting RTCI interrupts. Figure 9-14 shows the simplified flow-charts of the sections of the program concerned with interrupt service after the operator has depressed the "single sample" button and generated a SAMPI interrupt request. It is assumed that all IRQ interrupts are enabled and all but the SAMPI PIA interrupt lines are disabled. (All of the internal registers of the microprocessor are stacked away when an interrupt request is recognized. They are restored during execution of the return from interrupt instruction.)

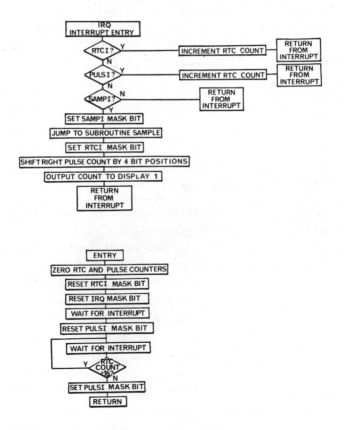

Figure 9-14. Program flow-charts for single shot measurement of count rate

The interrupt control program accounts for approximately 300 bytes of program memory.

In this application the data analysis is performed using two's complement binary integer arithmetic with intermediate scaling checks. The main estimation program is approximately 1 kbyte in length and requires six extended-precision arithmetic routines:

(i)   A three-byte binary addition routine.

(ii)   A three-byte binary subtraction routine.

(iii) A three-byte by three-byte signed binary multiplication routine.

(iv) A six-byte by three-byte unsigned binary divide routine.

(v)   A five-byte square-root routine.

(vi) A two-byte natural logarithm routine.

Together with a utility routine to transfer n-byte binary numbers between different locations in the data store, the arithmetic routines require some 600 bytes of additional program memory.

System development techniques. The program was written in 6800 assembler mnemonics and translated into hexadecimal machine code using a cross-assembler executed on a large IBM 360 computer system. During program development, pin-compatible RAM chips replaced all but one of the PROM chips in the program memory of the instrument. The remaining PROM chip held the vector of interrupt trap addresses. The application program was loaded into the program memory via the teletype and under the control of the software debug program. The "reset" interrupt trap address was initially set to cause execution of the debug program whenever the system was reset during program development. After the application program had been completely tested it was dumped into paper-tape via the teletype and loaded into the fusible-link PROM's using an off-line paper-tape PROM-Programmer. The PROM's were then substituted for the RAM chips in the program memory. Finally, the ACIA, the debug PROM and the teletype were disconnected from the instrument and the "reset" trap address reset to point to the start of the application program.

To test complete microprocessor-based instruments it is frequently convenient, and sometimes essential, to write a high level language version of the data analysis section of the microprocessor program which can be run on a large computer system. Using artificially generated input data, the output from this numerically accurate version of the program can provide comparative data to verify the basic analysis technique and to check the results and the accuracy of the microprocessor program.

THE BUY OR MAKE DECISION

Microprocessors offer the possibility of very low cost general-purpose computers. Several manufacturers offer ready-built or half-built computers based on well-known microprocessors. The microprocessor user is faced with the decision whether to buy a ready-made system for his application or to construct one in-house. As a rough guideline it is estimated that, where the total number of units to be constructed is less than 100, then it is certainly cost-effective to buy the complete system. For between 100 and 250 units the decision is less clear-cut, and above 250 units the user should consider designing and building his own system.

In the same way as microprocessor manufacturers offer ready-built computers based on their products, the companies specialising in A/D conversion offer complete analog subsystems which plug into the popular microcomputer chassis. The make or buy decision for analog subsystems is much the same as described above, except that the design and management of analog circuits at printed circuit board level is rather more difficult than that for digital circuits and requires different expertise. Consequently it is even more desirable to buy ready-made analog interfaces for micro-computers and the break-points in the buy or make decision move towards higher numbers. This argument for buying ready-built analog subsystems is particularly applicable for systems companies which use the microcomputer as a cheap solution to a particular applications problem.

Figure 9-15 shows the system diagram for a general-purpose analog subsystem which plugs into the Intel SBC80/10 series of computers based on the 8080 microprocessor. The input circuit consists of a 16-channel analog multiplexer, which feeds through a programmable gain amplifier to a sample-and-hold amplifier and thence to a

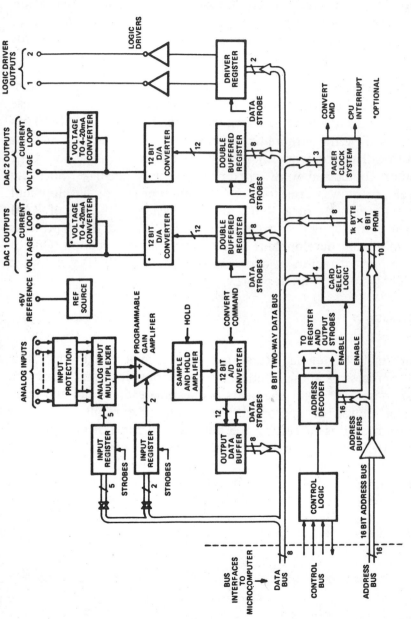

Figure 9-15. RTI 1200 analog interface circuit for Intel SBC computer

12-bit A/D converter. The output circuits consist of two double-buffered 12-bit D/A converters. Note that the system also includes a programmable real-time clock (called pacer clock by the manufacturer) because most microprocessors with analog interfaces require this feature. The reader is referred to the manufacturer for a full description of the system.

Finally, a word of warning. Although microprocessor-based computers offer low cost computing power, it is important to recognise that they do not offer low cost software. The Intel SBC80/10 has been used by the authors to drive automatic integrated-circuit test fixtures. The programs for driving the test fixtures use about 4K memory bytes and were written in assembly language. Software development was done on an Intel microprocessor development system consisting of a VDU, an 8080 system with 32K of RAM and a twin floppy disc drive. It is considered that this represents the minimum development hardware for this application. One of the important factors in choosing the Intel SBC80/10 was that it has extensive software support.

SUMMARY

This final chapter has attempted to give some insight into how microprocessors are used and the engineering decisions which the user must take. Most engineers over-estimate the speed and computing power of microprocessors and, as a result, encounter severe problems in getting the software to run fast enough. The best advice which can be offered is that, all other factors being equal (which they never are), one should use the most powerful microprocessor that the system can afford. (Friends have suggested that nothing less than an IBM 370 would satisfy the authors.)

APPENDIX

BIBLIOGRAPHY

The references listed here have appeared in the form of books, manuals, brochures, and articles in technical publications. Individual items have been selected because of their general or specific interest, or because they "fan out" through additional references not included here.

The list is representative rather than comprehensive and is heavily weighted in favor of recently-published material. In most cases, the practical has been preferred to the theoretical. Within each subject grouping, the titles are listed alphabetically.

The interested reader should, in any event, seek to obtain catalogs and application notes (often voluminous) from manufacturers of devices of interest. Lists of current manufacturers, their products, and their addresses, will be found in such industry guides as EEM and the Electronics Buyer's Guide. Since the technology is rapidly expanding (and changing), one should also seek to be placed on manufacturer's mailing lists, and to subscribe to at least one of the major semimonthly electronics industry technical periodicals to keep up with new products, new techniques, and new literature.

Readers of this book are invited to subscribe to Analog Dialogue, which appears (approximately) quarterly, and is available at no charge from Analog Devices, Inc.

GENERAL INFORMATION

Industrial Applications of Microprocessors, IEEE Conference, Trans. IEEE, Vol. IECI-22, No. 3, August 1975.

Industrial Applications of Microprocessors: Process Measurement and Failure-mode Analysis, IEEE Conference, Trans. IEEE, Vol. IECI-23, No. 3, August 1976.

An Introduction to Microcomputers, Osborne & Associates, 1976.

Introduction to Microcomputers and Microprocessors, A. Barna & D. I. Porat, Wiley-Interscience, 1976.

Introduction to Microprocessors, Ed. D. Aspinall & E. L. Dagless, Pitman/Academic, 1977.

Microcomputer Design, D. P. Martin, Martin Research Ltd., 1974.

Microcomputer Dictionary and Guide, C. J. Sippl & D.A. Kidd, Matrix, 1976.

Microcomputers – Fundamentals and Applications, Miniconsultant Ltd., 1975.

Microcomputers/Microprocessors: Hardware, Software and Applications, J. L. Hilburn & P. M. Julich, Prentice-Hall, 1976.

Microprocessors, Ed. L. Altman, McGraw-Hill, 1975.

Microprocessors (Quarterly), Guildford IPC Science & Technology Press, Vol. 1, No. 1, September 1976.

Microprocessors and Microcomputers, B. Souček, Wiley-Interscience, 1976.

Microprocessor Applications Bibliography, Ed. K. D. Mayne & J. E. Pache, IEE Library, 1975.

Microprocessor Applications Manual, McGraw-Hill, 1975.

Microprocessors at Work, SERT Symposium, 1976.

Microprocessors Technology, Architecture and Applications, D. R. McGlynn, Wiley-Interscience, 1976.

Minicomputers and Microprocessors, M. Healey, Hodder & Stoughton, 1976.

ARCHITECTURE AND MICROPROGRAMMING

A Bit-Slice Architecture for Microprogrammable Machines, M. Andrews, IEEE 9th Annual Workshop on Microprogramming, 1976.

A Computer Control Unit Using the Am 2909, J. R. W. Clymer, Advanced Micro Devices, Inc., 1975.

Computer System Architecture, M. M. Mano, Prentice-Hall, 1976.

Design of Microprogrammable Systems, New Electronics, May 1974.

Designing the Maximum Performance into Bit-Slice Minicomputers, G. F. Muething, Jr., Electronics, Vol. 49, No. 20, September 1975.

Intel Series 3000 Microprogramming Manual, Intel Corp., 1976.

Microarchitecture of Computer Systems, Ed. R. Hartenstein & R. Zaks, Eisevier, 1975.

Microcomputer Architecture: Memory and I/O Sections, L. A. Leventhal, Simulation, Vol. 28, No. 1, January 1977.

Microprogrammable Computer Architectures, A. B. Salisbury, Elsevier, 1976.

LSI MEMORY AND LOGIC

CCD's in Memory Systems Move into Sight, H. B. Crouch, J. C. Cornett & R. S. Eward, Computer Design 15, September 1976.

Components of Computers, F. F. Mazda, Electrochemical Publications, 1975.

The Biggest Erasable PROM yet puts 16384 Bits on a Chip, R. Greene, G. Perlegos, P. J. Salisbury & W. L. Morgan, Electronics, Vol. 50, No. 5, March 1977.

Design Techniques for Microprocessor Memory Systems, A. T. Thomas, Computer Design 14, August 1975.

Digital Design with Standard MSI and LSI, T. R. Blakeslee, Wiley-Interscience, 1975.

Hardware Multiplication Techniques for Microprocessor Systems, B. Parasuraman, Computer Design 16, April 1977.

How to Expand a Microcomputer's Memory, H. Raphael, Electronics, Vol. 49, No. 26, December 1976.

How to Use Dynamic Random Access Memories in a Microprocessor Environment, G. Debruyne, Intel Corp., 1975.

Integrated Circuits in Digital Electronics, A. Barna and D. I. Porat, Wiley-Interscience, 1973.

Intel Memory Design Handbook, Intel Corp., 1975.

Interfacing Core Stores to Microprocessors, Plessey Memories Application Notes Pub. No. 4657, 1974.

MOS-LSI Design and Application, W. N. Carr & J. P. Mize, McGraw-Hill, 1972.

A Non-Volatile Microprocessor Memory Using 4K N-Channel MOS RAMs, Motorola Application Note AN-732, 1974.

Physics of Computer Memory Devices, S. Middelhoek, P. K. George & P. Dekker, Academic Press, 1976.

PLAs Enhance Digital Processor Speed and Cut Component Count, G. Reyling, Electronics, Vol. 47, August 1974.

Semiconductor Memories, L. Altman, Electronics, Vol. 50, No. 2, January 1977.

A Shared Memory Technique for Different Microprocessors, R. L. Krutz and B. Reynouard, IEEE Conference, Parallel Processing, Proc. IEEE, Vol. 62, August 1976.

Special Issue on Semiconductor Memory and Logic, Trans. IEEE, Vol. SC-11, No. 5, October 1976; Vol. SC-10, No. 5, October 1975; and Vol. SC-8, No. 5, October 1973.

Trends in Computer Hardware Technology, D. A. Hodges, Computer Design 15, February 1976.

DIGITAL INTERFACES

A Peripheral Orientated Microcomputer System, J. E. Bass, Proc. IEEE, Vol. 64, No. 6, 1976.

Analysis of Multiple-Microprocessor System Architectures, A.J. Weissberger, Computer Design 16, June 1977.

Digital Interface Design, D. Zissos & F. G. Duncan, Oxford University Press, 1973.

Interfacing Peripherals in Mixed Systems, R. Moffa, Computer Design 14, April 1975.

Microcomputer Interfaces: Implementation and Problems, S. S. Weinrich & D. A. Cassell, IEEE International Symposium on Circuits and Systems, 1975.

Microprocessor Chip Scans Keyboard without Hardware Interface, D. Hammond, Electronics, Vol. 50, June 1977.

Microprocessor Interfaces, D. Zissos & F. G. Duncan, Electronic Letters, Vol. 12, No. 23, November 1976.

Operator's Console Considerations in Microprocessor System Design, J. Little & A. T. Thomas, Computer Design 14, November 1975.

Peripheral Interface Standards for Microprocessors, J. D. Nicoud, Proc. IEEE, Vol. 64, No. 6, 1976.

Trends in Intelligent Peripheral Chip Design, H. M. Bourne Jr., IEEE 13th Computer Society International Conference, September 1976.

ANALOG INTERFACES

A User's Handbook of D/A and A/D Converters, E. R. Hnatek, Wiley-Interscience, 1976.

An Integrated Approach to Analogue Interface Design, A. L. Dexter and R. G. Hayes, IEEE Conference Publication No. 127, Trends in On-Line Computer Control Systems.

A/D Conversion with the M6800, D. Aldridge, New Electronics, Vol. 9, No. 12, 1976.

Analog Output Chips Shrink A-D Conversion Software, A. Mrozowski, Electronics, Vol. 50, June 1977.

Analog-Digital Conversion Notes, Ed. D. H. Sheingold, Analog Devices, Inc., 1977.

Analog-to-Digital Conversion Techniques with the M6800 Microprocessor System, Motorola Application Note AN-757, 1975.

Analog-to-Digital Conversion Techniques, Motorola Application Notes AN-471, AN-559, AN-702, 1972–1974.

10-Bit Monolithic CMOS ADC Uses Fast Successive-Approximation Circuitry and is Compatible with Microprocessors, J. Whitmore & R. Van Aken, Analog Dialogue, Vol. 9, No. 2, 1975.

Distributed Microcomputer Data Acquisition, E. Y. Linn, J. D. Schoeffler & C.W. Rose, Instrumentation Technology, January 1975.

Interfacing Data Converters and Microprocessors, Fullagar et al., Electronics, Vol. 49, December 1976.

Interfacing the 8700 A/D Converter with the 8080 μP System, Teledyne Semiconductor Application Note No. 8, 1976.

Low Cost A-to-D Conversion During Microcomputer Idle Time, H. A. Raphael, Computer Design 16, March 1977.

Microcomputers for Data Acquisition, C. W. Rose & J. D. Schoeffler, Instrumentation Technology, September 1974.

Monolithic Sample/Hold Amplifiers: IC Flexibility Comes to the Sample/Hold Scene, D. Kress, Electronic Products, March 1977.

Monolithic 10-Bit CMOS Multiplying DAC Provides Direct Interface to Data Bus Inputs, J. Whitmore, Analogue Dialogue, Vol. 9, No. 3, 1975.

Problems of Analog Interface in Microprocessor-Based Systems, A. P. Brokaw, IEEE International Solid-State Circuits Conference, February 1976.

Software Controlled Analog-to-Digital Conversion, W. Ritmanich & W. Freeman, New Electronics, June 1977.

Versatile Analog-to-Microcomputer Interface, J. Fishbeck, Analogue Dialogue, Vol. 11, No. 1, 1977.

INDEX

A

B